The Battle for Municipal Reform

American Council On Public Affairs

Dedicated to the belief that the, extensive diffusion of information is a profound responsibility of American democracy, the American Council on Public Affairs is designed to promote the spread of authoritative facts and significant opinions concerning contemporary social and economic problems.

It endeavors to contribute to public knowledge through the publication of books, studies and pamphlets, encouragement of adult education, stimulation of interest in non-fiction materials, initiation of research projects, organization of lectures and forums, arrangement of radio broadcasts, issuance of timely press releases, compilation of opinions on vital issues, and cooperation with other organizations.

The Council believes that the facts presented and opinions expressed under its sponsorship deserve careful attention and consideration. It is not, however, committed to these facts and opinions in any other way. Those associated with the Council necessarily represent different viewpoints on public questions.

★ ★ ★ ★ ★ ★ ★ ★ ★ ★ ★ ★ ★

THE BATTLE FOR MUNICIPAL REFORM

Mobilization and Attack, 1875 to 1900

By Clifford W. Patton

★ ★ ★ ★ ★ ★ ★ ★ ★ ★ ★ ★ ★

Introduction

By Arthur M. Schlesinger

★ ★ ★ ★ ★ ★ ★ ★ ★ ★ ★ ★ ★

McGrath Publishing Company

College Park, Maryland

Reprint McGrath Publishing Company 1969
Library of Congress Catalog Card Number: 71-100458

Manufactured in the United States of America
by Arno Press, Inc., New York

Introduction

THE twentieth century opened a new chapter in the history of American cities. In these last four decades have occurred practically all the great constructive advances in municipal government: the short ballot, non-partisan elections, the divorce of city and general elections, municipal home rule, simplified frameworks of government, proportional representation, zoning regulations, city planning and the establishment of bureaus of municipal research. In 1900 not a single city had the commission-manager plan; now it has spread to more than four hundred and fifty communities. By the same token, four-fifths of the country's municipal employees are now under the merit system of appointment. Utopia has not yet arrived; but the nation's principal metropolis—no longer "America's most troublesome insular dependency"—enjoys the best government it has ever known, and everywhere the boss and the machine are finding the problem of survival increasingly difficult.

Professor Patton turns his searchlight on the dark ages that preceded this dawn—a period which provoked James Bryce's famous observation that municipal government was "the one conspicuous failure of the United States," and which occasioned Andrew D. White's confirmatory comment: "With very few exceptions, the city governments of the United States are the worst in Christendom—the most expensive, the most inefficient, and the most corrupt." The root of the difficulty lay in the fact that the American people, traditionally rural in outlook and governmental experience, had to start from scratch in learning how to administer densely packed urban centers.

It was not an art that could be mastered overnight even with the best of will; and in the case of many persons the will was lacking. Either they were indifferent, being engrossed in their own personal interests, or they were intent on using the municipal government to further their own personal interests. Rapid city growth meant an unprecedented expansion of public utilities—of water supply, rapid transit, and gas and electric lighting—as well as the public construction of streets, sewers and the like. "Where the carcass is," wrote Francis Parkman in 1878, "the vultures gather together." Predatory men, allying themselves with crooked politicians, obtained franchises, contracts and other special privileges with no safeguards for the paramount interests of the community. The complex form of municipal government, generally modeled on that of the state, facilitated these raids on the public weal.

1

In his first two chapters Professor Patton sets forth with illuminating detail the underlying reasons for the sorry state of municipal morals in the 1870's and 1880's. In the third chapter he discusses the rumblings of protest and the recurrent attempts of reform groups to replace corrupt officials with honest ones. Even when these efforts were successful, they accomplished little because, as the author makes clear, they were actuated by no fundamental or ultimate aim other than to "turn the rascals out." The next four chapters deal with the 1890's, which Professor Patton characterizes as the "great era of reform." By this time civic leaders had come to realize that their function was not merely to criticize and purge: they must also offer constructive proposals and show the way to permanent betterment of conditions. Contributions to this end came from many sources—from publicists such as E. L. Godkin and Gamaliel Bradford; from clergymen Josiah Strong and Samuel L. Loomis; from Jane Addams, Robert A. Woods and other social workers; from Jacob A. Riis, the police-court reporter who unsheathed his pen against the slum evil; and from public-spirited citizens in many walks of life.

Professor Patton is less concerned with whence came the ideas than with what results they achieved. He traces the progress attained during the closing decade in better municipal administration, better living conditions for the people, and better governmental machinery. From the standpoint of what had gone before, the ten years may rightly be regarded as a "great era of reform." From the standpoint of today, however, the decade has a different significance. It was a period of new beginnings, of pioneering and experiment, which prepared the way for the far greater advances of the twentieth century. The accomplishments of the crusaders of the 1890's formed the seedbed of later municipal reform as well as the training ground of leadership.

For this, if for no other reason, Professor Patton's little volume deserves careful perusal by students of government. It also merits the attention of historians, who have generally neglected urban history in their view of the American past. Nowhere else are the salient facts so conveniently presented or so cogently analyzed.

ARTHUR M. SCHLESINGER

Professor of History
Harvard University
Cambridge, Mass.

Preface

BOOKS on municipal government we have had in good number, even histories of the cities, but of the early years of the battle for municipal reform I know of no other single study which approaches the subject from the angle adopted in this volume.

This book had its origin in Professor Arthur M. Schlesinger's seminar at Harvard University, and has grown out of later reflections upon parts of the original project. My first thanks, therefore, is to Professor Schlesinger, whose teaching and writings have awakened a widespread interest in social and intellectual history. I wish to express gratitude also to the administration of the Oklahoma Baptist University for granting me a leave of absence, and to my colleagues who took over some of my teaching duties during that time. Many profitable hours have I spent talking with officials and scholars in various bureaus, libraries, and universities, all of whom have made contributions too numerous to specify. My indebtedness to the works of other writers is most apparent, and I trust sufficient recognition of their help appears in the footnotes and the bibliography. My immediate thanks is due to the American Council on Public Affairs for its interest in my efforts and especially to Mr. M. B. Schnapper, executive secretary of the Council, who has seen the manuscript through the press with surprising patience.

The bibliography, although by no means exhaustive, is, I believe, sufficiently complete not only to please those who venerate scholarship but also —and more especially—to be of use to any who may be bent upon a further pursuit of the subject. Additional information is easily accessible in the reports of numerous investigating committees and in the pages of popular and professional journals and newspapers of the period. Much pertinent material remains untouched.

In the terminology of 1940 this work is an historical study of a specific struggle for the enlistment of public opinion. The battle for civic reform was, in the final analysis, a battle against political ignorance and apathy— a battle for an enlightened public conscience. It took a long time to persuade John Q. that he had to fight. Crusaders and pressure groups armed themselves with propaganda techniques—of a sort—and set out to arouse a dormant and irresponsible electorate. The movement began with sporadic protests against extravagance, graft, and entrenched corruption. Then, between fitful waves of enthusiasm, the reformers sat down to rest while their enemies jumped on the bandwagon and rode back into office on the crest of public sentiment.

It is little short of a miracle that the reform movement did not die of a weak heart; and it is a matter of real significance to students of public opinion that gradually, by trial and error, the people's cause learned how to mobilize its strength, how to define the issues, how to strike at the fundamental weaknesses of municipal government. The founding of the National Municipal League in 1894 is indicative of a widespread interest in planned programs of civic betterment. By the turn of the century reform forces were prepared to look beyond the problems of petty machine politics to such larger goals as the strengthening of municipal charters, the effective control of finance, home rule, the scientific study of public health, and the education of a genuine civic conscience.

This is the story of that slow awakening of public interest in the battle for municipal reform. It is a heartening story to all who believe in the inherent potentialities of the American democratic system.

CLIFFORD W. PATTON

Professor of History and Government
Oklahoma Baptist University
Shawnee, Oklahoma

Contents

Enright in the *New York World-Telegram*

An Irresistible Force Takes Form

CHAPTER ONE

Basic Conditions and Causes

"THERE is no denying that the government of cities is the one conspicuous failure of the United States. The deficiences of the national government tell but little for evil on the welfare of the people. The faults of the state government are insignificant compared with the extravagance, corruption, and mismanagement which mark the administrations of most of the great cities."[1] Such is the oft-quoted accusation of our English critic, James Bryce, who in 1888 completed a thorough and searching study of the American commonwealth.

The statement was stern and harsh; there was no qualifying clause. And Bryce was right. One cannot review the trend of our municipalities from 1875 to 1900 without recognizing that, whatever improvements may be recorded to their credit, they were still a pitiful failure. They were like undisciplined children who had outgrown the simple standards of childhood and were groping helplessly for some adequate plan of life by which they could be at peace with themselves. For, while their failure is true, their bewildered and searching attempts at reform are equally true. There were proud and earnest citizens whose sense of justice and decency rebelled against the weakness and corruption of their city governments. Although their struggles at reform were often misguided and ineffectual, they were marked at times with substantial victories. As the student of today looks back upon the period, he finds in the work of its reformers an importance that he had not anticipated. The beginning of America's battle for municipal reform is arresting and significant in almost every detail.

What, then, were the conditions that gave rise to reform movements? Why were the cities of 1875 such a conspicuous failure? These questions are not easy to answer. Some would lay the blame at the door of a low public morality, resulting in an indifferent electorate and a corrupt administration. Others, searching deeper, find a more vital trouble in the framework itself of city government, which simply cracked under the excessive strain of a score of other faults. It will be profitable to review thoroughly the conditions that best explain the problems in question.

---

[1] Bryce, James, *The American Commonwealth* (New York, 1888), vol. 1, p. 608.

In the first place, America's cities were by 1875 well advanced in the amazing growth and complexity of the industrial revolution. The years following the Civil War saw spectacular railroad expansion[2] and a shift of the rural population to the centers of industry.[3] The nation was becoming more and more urbanized. While in 1860 there were 144 cities in the United States with a population of more than 8,000, by 1880 the number had increased to 285, and they had almost doubled again by 1900.[4] Where a generation before a city had been a simple institution, it suddenly awoke to find itself burdened with a population for which it was entirely unprepared. Its people were indifferent and untrained, its charter inadequate, its politicians only too eager to step in and profit by the confusion. It was not unusual for a city to double its population in a decade.[5] Small wonder, then, that the 1870's found American city government at its lowest ebb.[6]

With the sudden increase in population came a mad scramble for public improvements. The newcomers must have places to live, water and gas for their homes, street cars to take them to their work. The streets were continually being torn up for water mains, sewerage lines, or paving projects.[7] While the tremendous assets of such expansion are obvious— making life more comfortable, knitting city and country together, and improving the welfare of the people as a whole—they were put into effect in such a way as to seriously endanger good government.

With the rise of the public utility the city willingly granted liberal franchises and subsidies to corporations whose later struggle for monopoly

---

[2] Between 1870 and 1880 railway mileage increased from 52,922 miles to 93,-261 miles. In 1890 it reached 167,191 miles, and by 1900, 198,964 miles. Faulkner, Harold Underwood, *American Economic History* (New York, 1925), pp. 452, 453.

[3] In 1850, 12.49% of the total population of the United States lived in cities of more than 8,000; by 1880 the percentage had increased to 22.57. Weber, A. F., *The Growth of Cities in the Nineteenth Century* (New York, 1899), p. 22. From 1870 to 1900 the population of breadwinners engaged in trade, transportation, and professional service increased from 13% to 21%. Weber, A. F., "Rapid Transit and The Housing Problem," *Municipal Affairs*, vol. 6 (Fall, 1902), p. 410. From 1860 to 1870 manufacturing establishments increased 79%. Orth, Samuel Peter, *The Boss and the Machine* (Allen Johnson, ed., *The Chronicles of America Series*, vol. 43, New Haven, 1920), p. 36.

[4] Faulkner, *op. cit.*, p. 584.

[5] From 1880 to 1890 Birmingham gained 245%; Los Angeles, 211%; Seattle, 194%; Spokane, 183%; Dallas, 116%; Schenectady, 129%. By 1890 there were six cities with 500,000 or more, 15 with more than 200,000, and 28 with more than 100,000. Orth, *op. cit.*, p. 52. The population in the eight leading cities increased 24% from 1870 to 1880; 119% from 1880 to 1890. Weber, Gustavus A., "Improved Tenement Homes for American Cities," *Municipal Affairs*, vol. 1 (December, 1897), p. 745.

[6] Griffith, Ernest S., *The Modern Development of City Government in the United Kingdom and in the United States* (London, 1927), vol. 1, p. 20.

[7] *Ibid.*, p. 79.

brought bribery and graft into local government. Improvement programs might have been accomplished with less harm had there been some strong supervising agency, but, as it was, every board and commission joined the scuffle to fight for its own unscrupulous ends. Each new city development "brought grist to the politician's mill."[8] W. M. Evarts, chairman of a commission set up to devise a plan of government for New York in 1876, reported that the money already spent on paving, piers, sewers, and buildings would have been sufficient to care for city progress for years to come, but that the type of work was so inferior that it was only money wasted and misapplied.[9] The municipality was not prepared for its new responsibility; out of the growth of functions arose only disorganization, confusion, incoherence.

Most alarming of the public utility problems was that of rapid transit. Franchises for street railways, omnibus lines, and ferries had been granted while the cities were still in their infancy. Now as the population increased and the streets and traffic multiplied, competition arose between the transit companies and monopoly inevitably followed. While the street railway industry had been small prior to 1870 and limited to horse railway lines in a few large cities, improvements in motive power from 1870 to 1880 brought street railways to most cities of reasonable size.[10] The excitement that arose during this decade—the San Francisco cars were then equipped with a cable system—was a mild forerunner of the storm that was soon to strike American cities with the rapid expansion of electric traction from 1885 to 1897.[11] Extravagant estimates of future profit served as the basis for extravagant ideas of capitalization. Syndicates were formed to purchase horse railways and equip them with electricity.[12]

And through the whole story of expansion runs a trail of fraud and unfair privilege. The New York Elevated Railroad Company, chartered in 1875, paid the city only five percent annually until 1890 and then refused further payment. When the city tried to force payment through a court battle in 1894, it failed because of a legal technicality. The elevated company that entered Brooklyn in 1888 obtained a franchise that cost

[8] Orth, *op. cit.*, p. 59.

[9] Foulke, William Dudley, "Coming of Age: Municipal Progress in Twenty-One Years," *National Municipal Review*, vol. 5 (January, 1916), pp. 12, 13.

[10] Higgins, Edward E., "Municipal and Private Management of Street Railways—A Study of Results and Possibilities," *Municipal Affairs*, vol. 1 (September, 1897), p. 465.

[11] According to Clayton C. Hall the first regularly equipped electric railway in America was opened in Baltimore on August 10, 1885. Hall, Clayton C., *Baltimore: Its History and Its People* (New York, 1912), p. 549. For Richmond's claim to the first electric street railway see Schlesinger, Arthur M., *The Rise of the City 1878-1898* (Arthur M. Schlesinger and Dixon Ryan Fox, eds., *A History of American Life*, vol. 10, New York, 1933), p. 92.

[12] Higgins *loc. cit.*, p. 465.

nothing and, at the same time, was required to pay no license fee.[13] New York City's experiences with the street railway were none too fortunate. The municipality granted its first street railway franchise in 1851, but the laws were later repealed. In 1875 the state passed the Rapid Transit Act, requiring that franchises for street railways be granted by the state legislature only. One cannot help questioning the probity of that legislature when one reads the exposure of the franchise reported by New York City's Reform Club. For it was the Reform Club, through its Committee on City Affairs, that revealed, among other schemes, the famous Broadway franchise scandal of 1884, when Jacob Sharp obtained the franchise for a song.[14]

The public utility question carried with it the temptation of municipal ownership. Most of the large cities owned their own water works, a few their own gas works. What a harvest for the politicians! As early as 1842, New York City had completed the Croton Aqueduct, 38 miles long, the largest in the world. With the growth of the city, a new aqueduct became necessary and was authorized in 1883. It was built at a cost of $35,000,000, but its defective work revealed the immense profit that must have been pocketed by corrupt officials.[15] It was Philadelphia's ownership of the gas works, which the city bought from a private company in 1841, that gave rise to an unscrupulous political ring centering in the gas trust.[6] Practically all of Philadelphia's later municipal problems can be blamed directly upon the machine politics of Boss James McManes and the gas trust.[17]

As a result of the extravagance, inefficiency, and fraud of ventures in public improvements, the cities found themselves, by 1875, hopelessly swamped by debt. In the seven years between 1868 and 1875, 15 cities having a population increase of 71% showed a debt increase of 271%. Cleveland's indebtedness increased 355%. New York City showed a debt in 1876 of $113,000,000. Philadelphia had a debt of $61,000,000 in 1878.[18] With the changes in purchasing power that resulted from the panic of

---

[13] Conkling, Alfred Ronald, *City Government in the United States* (New York, 1899), pp. 112-114.
[14] Reform Club Committee on City Affairs, "Street Railway Franchises in New York," *Municipal Affairs*, vol. 6 (March, 1902), pp. 81, 82.
[15] Conkling, *op. cit.*, pp. 95, 96.
[16] *Ibid.*, pp. 102-105.
[17] New York papers in 1876 reported that the gas ring had stolen $8,-000,000 from the city of Philadelphia in the last few years. Nevins, Allan, *The Emergence of Modern America 1865-1878* (Arthur M. Schlesinger and Dixon Ryan Fox, eds., *A History of American Life*, vol. 8, New York, 1927), p. 313.
[18] Griffith, *op. cit.*, p. 64; Allinson, Edward Pease, and Penrose, Boies, *Philadelphia 1681-1887: A History of Municipal Development* (Philadelphia, 1887), p. 241.

1873, the price level fell 34% by 1878 and city debts became staggering.[19]

It is interesting to note the comparative figures of state and municipal indebtedness by 1880, for they suggest that, except in the Southern states, there was far more extravagance and misrule in city finance than in state finance.[20] The census of 1880 shows a total state indebtedness of $259,-964,045 and a city and town indebtedness of $765,875,258. Most of the debts in the Southern cities were caused by the heavy loans they had made to private corporations. It is estimated that in 1870 Southern cities carried a loan of $185,000,000 for the aid of private enterprise.[21] Connecticut found itself in something of the same position in 1875 with municipal debts of $13,995,000, one-third of which had gone to the railroads; the state legislature presented a Constitutional amendment to restrict cities from aiding railroad corporations, but the amendment failed.[22]

We have so far traced the evils of rapid city growth through the normal sequence of industrialization, civic improvements, public utilities, municipal ownership, and debt. There was another contributing factor which, if not responsible for all the crimes laid at its door, certainly did add to the complexity and difficulty of the situation. This was the matter of immigration. To just what extent immigration was responsible for the ills of the city is a debatable question, and one that deserves further study. Most of the foreigners who entered the United States in the late nineteenth century were attracted to the cities, which offered such visible advantages as employment, parks, concerts, and charities.[23] New York

---

[19] Griffith, *op. cit.*, pp. 62, 63; *World Almanac for 1923*, p. 121. In spite of the fall in prices, the cost of city government in New York, Baltimore, Boston, and Detroit advanced 11.2% from 1870 to 1880. Griffith, *op. cit.*, p. 63.

	State Indebtedness	City and Town Indebtedness
[20] *New England*	$ 49,950,926	$146,304,767
Vermont	4,000	4,223,942
Massachusetts	33,034,726	87,223,947
Middle States	44,604,511	407,374,756
New York	8,988,360	217,825,069
Pennsylvania	21,561,990	100,054,742
Western States	39,710,453	135,501,703
Southern States	125,728,155	76,696,032
Total	$259,994,045	$765,877,258

Kasson, John A., "Municipal Reform," *North American Review*, vol. 137 (September, 1883), pp. 218-220.

[21] Griffith, *op. cit.*, p. 65.

[22] "The Prevention of Local Extravagance," *Nation*, vol. 21 (July 8, 1875), pp. 21-23.

[23] In 1873, 459,803 immigrants entered the United States. By 1882 the number increased to 788,922 for the one year, and in 1900 we received more than 850,000. Faulkner, *op. cit.*, p. 612.

City received the greatest number; in 1870, 44% of her population was foreign-born.[24] While many immigrants were, of course, good and useful citizens, the majority were ignorant and credulous, unaccustomed to the privilege of the ballot, and with no conception of the true aims of municipal government. The mixture of so many nationalities, the lack of homogeneity, made the problem of city government infinitely more difficult.[25]

The chief trouble in connection with the effect of immigration on city government was the fact that many foreigners were easily influenced and easily bought by local politicians. It became a common practice for "ward heelers" to supervise the naturalization of foreigners in their districts and then herd them to the polls to support the political machine.[26] As early as 1854 Fernando Wood won the office of Mayor in New York City by his thorough organization of the foreign element. Boss Tweed, who succeeded Wood, bolstered his influence with the immigrants by finding jobs for his constituents, by helping the fellow in trouble with the law, and by lavishly distributing charities and free coal in the winter time.[27] After the Tweed Ring was overthrown in 1871, the people again became neglectful of their voting rights, and Tammany Hall came into power, with John Kelley as boss, on the strength of the foreign vote.[28]

One cannot mention the problem of the foreigner in American city life without thinking of the peculiar place that the Irishman has occupied. One writer has gone so far as to say, "The function of the Irishman is to administer the affairs of the American city."[29] Between 1840 and 1890 our Irish immigrants numbered 3,250,000, more than half of whom settled in the cities, and one-fourth of whom flocked to New York, Brooklyn, Chicago, Boston, and Philadelphia. In 1886 one-seventh of the population of New York City was Irish. For many years the Irish have furnished not merely a large percentage of the electorate but also most of the political leadership of New York, Brooklyn, Jersey City, Hoboken, Boston, Chicago, Buffalo, Albany, Troy, Pittsburgh, St. Paul, St. Louis, Kansas City, Omaha, New Orleans, and San Francisco. They lost out in Indianapolis, Providence and Philadelphia simply because they fell into opposing groups. Milwaukee and Cincinnati, on the other hand, were under German-American control.[30]

---

[24] Bryce, op. cit. (1911 edition), vol. 2, p. 380.

[25] Devlin, Thomas C., Municipal Reform in the United States (New York, 1896), p. 22.

[26] Orth, op. cit., p. 61.

[27] Godkin, E. L., "Criminal Politics," North American Review, vol. 150 (June, 1890), pp. 711, 712; Nevins, op. cit., p. 185.

[28] Bryce, op. cit. (1911 edition), vol. 2, p. 396.

[29] Bocock, John Paul, "The Irish Conquest of Our Cities," Forum, vol. 17 (April, 1894), p. 186.

[30] Ibid., pp. 186-188.

While it is obvious that immigration added its share to the difficulties of municipal government in the period from 1875 to 1900, it would be a grave inaccuracy and injustice to claim that it was the major evil. In defense of the immigrant it has been shown that Philadelphia, with a greater percentage of native Americans than any other large city, was the most corrupt, and that San Francisco reformers received some of their best aid from the Irish and the Germans.[31] Dr. Charles W. Eliot once said, "The great majority of the immigrants have been serviceable people . . . have had a better education than the average rural American can obtain . . . The theory that the immigration of a few millions of foreigners within thirty years is the true cause of municipal evils in the United States must also be rejected, although the too quick admission to the suffrage of men who have had no acquaintance with free institutions has doubtless increased the evils of city government in a few localities." [32]

Closely bound to all the ill effects of the rapid growth and industrialization of the cities was the spirit of the people themselves. "The country," in the opinion of Prof. Arthur M. Schlesinger, "was suffering from a general lowering of its moral tone, as a reaction from the lofty idealism of war days."[33] Energetic men were lured into the wild scramble for wealth; they had no time to think of civic responsibility. Our municipal system was arranged when most competent men could command the little leisure which public duty required. "Dr. Franklin, in the Convention of 1787, based his plan of government upon that fact. He said he could not doubt that it would always be possible to find in the United States men of leisure and public spirit to perform the simple duties which a rational republican government would impose."[34] But Franklin did not foresee the changes that the next century was to bring. The better class of men in the late nineteenth century were concerned primarily with their private business affairs.

In the second place, those men who did give time and thought to politics were interested chiefly in national and state issues. During and after the Civil War national questions became so absorbing that the bulk

[31] Faulkner, Harold Underwood, *The Quest for Social Justice 1898-1914* (Arthur M. Schlesinger and Dixon Ryan Fox, eds., *A History of American Life*, vol. 11, New York, 1931), p. 92; Older, Mrs. Fremont, "The Story of a Reformer's Wife," *McClure's Magazine*, vol. 33 (1909), pp. 292, 293. "The immigrant was often blamed for the sorry conditions of affairs, but outside New York City the bosses and grafting politicians were usually of native stock." Schlesinger, *op. cit.*, p. 392.

[32] Eliot, Charles W., "One Remedy for Municipal Misgovernment," *Forum*, vol. 12 (October, 1891), p. 155.

[33] Schlesinger, Arthur M., *Political and Social History of the United States 1829-1925* (New York, 1925), p. 289.

[34] Parton, James, "Municipal Government," *Chautauquan*, vol. 8 (January, 1888), p. 204.

of the people hardly considered city affairs. The same man to whom the
issues at Washington seemed vital had not yet awakened to the disastrous
problems of his own community. The needs of the city were blindly
neglected by those intelligent citizens who might have solved them. When
an emergency arose, some haphazard and temporary solution was all that
was offered.[35] City elections were held at the time of national elections
and on the same blanket ballot. Candidates for city offices campaigned
on a platform of tariff. And the public was hard put to make clear dis-
tinctions.

Into the gap left by an indifferent electorate stepped the political
boss and his machine, ready to fill their pockets as the donors of appointments and the allies of big business.[36] Political scandals were not limited
to the cities. State and national politics were at the same low ebb. Legislatures bowed obediently to corporations, obediently, as long as they were
well paid. Governor Tilden of New York reported in 1876 the overthrow
of the Canal Ring, which had wasted or stolen $15,000,000. In the same
year the lobbyists of the horse railways defeated the Husted rapid transit
bill for Albany by purchasing votes at $250 to $1,500 each.[37] In 1871 the
Governor of Nebraska was removed for embezzlement. Kansas was
startled by bribery in her senatorial elections in 1872 and 1873. The halls
of Washington heard whispers of the Credit Mobilier affair, the Whiskey
Ring, the Belknap Scandal.[38]

We have considered, up to this point, the conditions of city life and
growth as they affected the conduct of municipal affairs. For a long time
that was all that people could see. When they bemoaned the corruption of
their cities, they pointed to growth and materialism as the primary causes.
From the vantage point of later years, however, one can see behind the
scenery a weak and inappropriate framework—a fundamental problem. The whole plan of city government in the United States was inadequate; it was not strong enough of itself to stand against the challenge of
normal modern expansion. "The municipal institutions . . . of most
American cities, from the very beginning, were founded upon an anti-
quated system, ill suited to modern times."[39] City charters were clumsy
and inappropriate, their legislative machinery weak, their executive
restricted, their courts unorganized. John C. Bullitt, author of the Philadelphia Bullitt Charter, once said, "If you would strike a real and effective
blow [at municipal abuses] then begin at the ultimate cause. Reform

[35] Foulke, *op. cit.*, p. 14.
[36] Howe, Frederic C., *The Modern City and Its Problems* (New York, 1915),
pp. 91-93.
[37] Nevins, *op. cit.*, p. 312.
[38] Orth, *op. cit.*, pp. 43-48.
[39] Allinson and Penrose, *op. cit.*, p. 259.

the framework of the government, and thus destroy that which germi-
nates and maintains them." [40]

The principal fault of most city charters was their inflexibility.
They "were not drawn on lines simple enough to permit easy internal
reorganization."[41] As new questions arose, amendments were hastily
added. The result was confusion and contradiction. The charter of Jersey
City was revised 91 times between 1835 and 1875.[42] The date of municipal
elections in St. Paul was changed three times in four years.[43]

Another serious defect of most of the charters was their failure to
fix responsibility. While the greatest power resided in the City Council,
there were so many boards and independently elected officials that, when
a controversy arose, the board involved blamed the Council, the Council
blamed the Mayor, and the Mayor blamed the state legislature. "There
was such an ingenious combination of checks and balances and mingling
of power, that nobody could be to blame for anything. It took everybody
to do anything, and everybody did it, and everybody said it was you and
not I, and everybody was right." [44]

The Councils, having assumed executive as well as legislative
functions, found it necessary to appoint a multiplicity of committees to
attend to administrative details. In some cases, independent boards were
elected by the people or appointed by the Mayor, and in a few cases
appointed by the Governor of the state. Their powers were ill defined,
there was no co-ordinating agency, they were not directly responsible to
anyone. Philadelphia at one time had 30 of these boards. The city had no
defense against the practice of favoritism in the awarding of contracts
and appointments, or the purchasing of supplies. A shrewd manipulator
could virtually control all municipal activities.[45]

Even the judicial functions of the municipal government were poorly
regulated by the charters. There was no uniformity within the states. In
most cases judicial offices were elective rather than appointive.[46] Where
machine politics controlled the ballot, it was simple enough for men to
fill the benches with their own followers. In New York City hardly one
in four of the police justices were lawyers; most were expert and unscru-

[40] *Ibid.*, p. 263.
[41] Griffith, *op. cit.*, p. 108.
[42] Lee, Francis Bazley, *New Jersey as a Colony and as a State* (New York,
1902), vol. 4, p. 243.
[43] Castle, Henry Anson, *History of St. Paul and Vicinity* (New York, 1912),
p. 177 ff.
[44] Bowles, Samuel, "Relation of State to Municipal Government and the Reform of the Latter," *Journal of Social Science*, vol. 9 (January, 1878), p. 142.
[45] Orth, *op. cit.*, pp. 55-57.
[46] In Maryland and Massachusetts, however, the Governor appointed the
police magistrates. Conkling, *op. cit.*, p. 84.

pulous politicians.[47] By 1894 New York had 15 police judges, each with an annual salary of $8,000.[48] Small wonder that fraud and vice went unmolested!

In short, the weakness of the form itself of city government was a more fundamental cause of civic ills than the complexities arising from rapid growth and a general low tone of public morality.

A third factor in the difficulties of the cities at this period was the excessive interference of the state in municipal affairs. The city was, after all, a creature of the state and it was quite natural for the city to turn for help to the higher authority which was the source of its charter. In many a critical emergency, state legislation had saved a city from disaster. Memphis, for example, was struggling under a $6,000,000 debt in 1876, inherited from the mismanagement of the previous administration. With the Yellow Fever epidemic in 1878, the city fell into bankruptcy and affairs were so entangled that in 1879 her charter was abolished and her administration placed in the hands of a commission appointed by the Governor.[49] Tradition in Tennessee was for local freedom, but when circumstances called for direct intervention, the state took the authority into her own hands and bridged the crisis.[50] The Pennsylvania legislature set up a barrier to Philadelphia's extravagance by the "Pay-As-You-Go Act" of 1879, according to which the city's appropriations must be kept within its income or the acts of the Council would become void.[51]

State legislation for the cities, then, was not harmful in itself; the difficulty at this time was that the legislatures were abusing their right of intervention and dictating to the cities in questions of purely local concern. "Accustomed to interfere in matters which were of interest to the state government, the legislature failed to distinguish between such matters and matters which were of main, if not of exclusive, interest to the cities themselves."[52] State interference had reached such an extent that the New York legislature passed more municipal laws in the three years

---

[47] Eaton, Dorman, B., *The Government of Municipalities* (New York, 1899), p. 437 ff.

[48] Conkling, *op. cit.*, p. 85.

[49] Malone, James H., "Municipal Conditions of Memphis, Tennessee," National Conference for Good City Government, *Proceedings for 1896*, pp. 111, 112.

[50] The city of Mobile, Alabama, went into bankruptcy in 1879 after the Yellow Fever epidemic and its extravagant attempts to compete with New Orleans in construction; the legislature repealed its charter and Mobile ceased to be a city, but was known only as a port. Brown, William G., *A History of Alabama* (New York, 1900), p. 291.

[51] Allinson and Penrose, *op. cit.*, p. 256. The authors record a debt of $73,615,351.79 in Philadelphia in 1878.

[52] Goodnow, Frank Johnson, *City Government in the United States* (New York, 1904), p. 57.

between 1867 and 1870 than the entire total in England for the 50 years from 1835 to 1885. There were 39 state laws for Brooklyn alone in 1870.[53] The Illinois Constitution for 1870 gave fairly broad powers to the cities, but Chicago was still unable to grant concessions for "checking hats or selling popcorn on the new municipal pier without a special act of the legislature!" [54]

The evils of such excessive state interference were almost without limit. In the first place, municipal affairs were occupying far too great a proportion of the legislature's time. The Fassett Committee reported 1,284 acts passed by the New York legislature for cities alone from 1880 to 1889.[55] Kentucky in 1890 passed 176 public acts and 1,752 private acts for cities.[56] In the second place, state legislators were not acquainted with the details of civic problems, nor did they have the time to investigate them thoroughly. Their information reached them largely from those who sought to satisfy their own personal gains. Such practices led to a third evil, corruption. Legislators found it convenient and profitable to exchange votes with one another in the interests of their local policies.[57] Or lobbyists contrived to spend the city's money against the protest of citizens and taxpayers. Communities were compelled by the legislature to make specific purchases for parks or streets. Mayor Lowe of Brooklyn said that every year he had to fight the legislature to keep it from raising the salaries of policemen and firemen.[58]

Another common form of corruption was called "ripper" legislation, by which an official who was threatened with defeat would have his tenure of office prolonged by an act of the legislature; or, if his post was to be abolished, he would have it placed under state control and thereby keep his name on the pay roll. New and useless offices were frequently created for just such a purpose as this. Thus it came about that state aid, which originally had been a necessity and a benefit to municipal growth, had been so abused as to add another serious complication to the ills of city government.

---

[53] Griffith, *op. cit.*, p. 22.
[54] Merriam, Charles Edward, *Chicago: A More Intimate View of Urban Politics* (New York, 1929), pp. 14, 15.
[55] Agar, John G., "Legislative Interference in New York," *Municipal Affairs*, vol. 6 (June, 1902), p. 210; Fassett Committee, *Testimony Taken Before the Senate Committees on Cities, Pursuant to Resolutions Adopted January 20, 1890* (Albany, 1890), vol. 4, p. 459.
[56] Griffith, *op. cit.*, p. 128.
[57] Bryce, *op. cit.*, vol. 1, p. 646.
[58] *Ibid.*, pp. 660, 661; Devlin, *op. cit.*, pp. 72, 73.

CHAPTER TWO

The Evils of Machine Politics

THE question of municipal conditions in 1875 resolves itself to this. The cities of the United States, faced with the problems of rapid growth and industrialization and relying upon an electorate that was occupied primarily in the scramble for wealth, found their whole plan of government inadequate and their welfare hampered by the interference of the state. The product of this confusion was a glaring display of corruption in the administrative forces. What greater advantages could the scheming politicians have asked than a broad program of civic improvements, an apathetic public, a weak charter that failed to fix responsibility, and a conniving legislature? The scene was perfectly set. Machine politics, graft, and party prejudice stepped in to profit by the confusion.

The central figure of machine politics was the party boss. He was the pivot around which revolved an obedient circle of "trusties," whose jobs in city offices were the reward for service to the party. In the early seventies bossism was experimental, but the next two decades saw it develop into a fine technique. It was the boss's chief delight to manage appointments so perfectly that no opposition could enter government circles. The boss controlled the nominating machinery and prepared the slate. If a reform Mayor slipped into office, he soon learned that he must bow to the boss or give up his own program as a failure. It was not an uncommon trick for the machine to "perfume the ticket" by supporting a good man for Mayor; their own candidates filled the rest of the slate.[1] There were schemes to satisfy every plot and keep the boss supreme. James McManes, leader of the gas trust ring in Philadelphia, was so annoyed by the honest administration of Mayor Edwin H. Fitler that he and his friend, Matthew S. Quay, marched off to the Republican National Convention in 1888 and nominated Fitler for President![2]

"Has the reader ever heard of the Pilgrim Club? If not, let

---

[1] Steffens, Lincoln, *The Shame of the Cities* (New York, 1904), p. 196 ff.
[2] *Ibid.*, pp. 197, 198. Fitler was the first Mayor under the new charter, 1887 to 1891, and helped to promote many reforms. Frederick, John H., "Edwin Henry Fitler," *Dictionary of American Biography*, vol. 6, pp. 431, 432.

him go back to the files of the [Philadelphia] *Times* of 1875-6,
and read there of the practices of mutually interested bosses,
Republican and Democrat, who were accustomed to meet together
in fraternal council and arrange their plans whereby each was to
do his part in the election, in the interest of certain of the candidates of the other, in return for which they would all have a share
in the profits of the respective offices."[3] Only the scathing
exposure of the "Pilgrims" in the Philadelphia papers served to
break up their friendly gatherings.

With the success of bossism, politics became a profession with
a certain swagger and style of its own. The boss and his subordinates were "good sports," fancy dressers. A contemporary
observer sardonically noted that "officialism" has "a fondness for
shining silk hats and heavy jewelry whereby those of its guild
may be distinguished apart from other citizens anywhere save as
regards one particular class known as 'gamblers' who not infre-
quently are confounded with them, not any more by reason of
similarity of personal appearance than by reason of a certain
resemblance as to loudness in the display of money and a reckless-
ness in spending it."[4]

The history of municipal government would be colorless
without the names of such clever bosses as Christopher L. Magee
of Pittsburgh, "Honest" John Kelley and Richard Croker of New
York, "King" James McManes of Philadelphia, "Czar" Martin
Lomasney of Boston, Ed Butler of St. Louis. Boss Magee became
City Treasurer of Pittsburgh in 1871; he studied the rings of New
York and Philadelphia until he and William Flinn perfected their
own machine in the city of "Hell with the lid off."[5] "Honest" John
Kelley, a stone mason, began his political career as sheriff in
1858 and rose to be dictator of Tammany Hall from 1874 to 1886.[6]
He it was who persuaded Samuel J. Tilden, August Belmont, and
Horatio Seymour to become his sachems.[7] Kelley controlled two
newspapers in New York City, the *Star* and the *Evening Express*.
In these he kept alive his influence. He ordered the Board of
Excise Commissioners not to grant a license to any saloon keeper

---

[3] Vickers, George, *The Fall of Bossism: A History of the Committee of One Hundred, and the Reform Movement in Philadelphia and Pennsylvania* (Phila-delphia, 1883), p. 37.
[4] *Ibid.*, p. 17.
[5] Steffens, *op. cit.*, pp. 147-164.
[6] Werner, M. R., *Tammany Hall* (Garden City, N. Y., 1928), p. 278.
[7] Orth, *The Boss and the Machine*, p. 81.

who did not subscribe for two paid-up subscriptions to the *Star*. Thus he contrived to keep opposition papers out of the saloons.[8]

The most shocking and dangerous consequence of machine politics was the graft which it entailed. Financial and moral interests of the city were sacrificed at every turn to personal gain. As Andrew D. White concluded in 1890, municipal government in the United States, in addition to being the most inefficient in Christendom, was, with few exceptions, the most expensive and the most corrupt.[9] Politicians rose in a few years from tenements to brown stone mansions, from humble trades to the boards of rich corporations.[10] Their revenue came as fees from favored office seekers, contractors, banks, railroads, public utilities, or as hush money from prostitutes and gamblers. The organized forces of vice paid well for the protection of the police. Bidding for contracts and franchises, while theoretically competitive, was reduced to a mere farce, usually by the arrangement of specifications so that none but the favored firm could bid successfully.[11]

Philadelphia could not boast that it was a clean Quaker city in 1880, for while large improvements were projected, there was not enough money in the treasury to clean the streets and the "City of Homes" was dubbed the "City of Dirt."[12] During the reign of "King" McManes the gas trust was accused of defrauding the people of $1,000 a day. When alert citizens attempted to investigate the books, their procedure was barred and the investigation died in a committee of the councils.[13]

One of Philadelphia's most profitable sources of funds for the machine was the office of the Collector of Delinquent Taxes, with a yearly profit of almost $200,000. This officer was appointed by the Receiver of Taxes, and oftimes the bosses of both parties secretly agreed that whichever side won in the receivership, the profits of the Collector of Delinquent Taxes would be pooled and divided among them.[14] The tax office became the graduating place for gas trustees and their enormous revenue was wrung from the

---

[8] Werner, *op. cit*, p. 283.

[9] White, A. D., "The Government of American Cities," *Forum*, vol. 10 (1891-1892), p. 357; Gregory, Charles N., *Civil Service Reform in American Municipalities* (Iowa City, 1905), pp. 4, 5.

[10] Vickers, *op. cit.*, p. 17.

[11] Griffith, *The Modern Development of City Government in the United Kingdom and in the United States*, p. 138. Mr. Griffith cites an example of a ring among contractors in Grand Rapids, Michigan, whereby they agreed in advance who should be the low bidder.

[12] Vickers, *op. cit.*, p. 19.

[13] *Ibid.*, pp. 162, 163.

[14] *Ibid.*, pp., 156-159.

poorer class of taxpayers who could not afford to pay and yet were unable to secure exemption.

Pittsburgh's story of graft is sordid and revolting. While corruption entered St. Louis from the financial circles at the top, and came to Minneapolis through the police at the bottom, Pittsburgh "got it" from both ends.[15] The worst frauds in Pittsburgh's record came from the rivalry of the railroad corporations, whom the city had once so eagerly welcomed and encouraged. The Pennsylvania Railroad, according to Lincoln Steffens, purchased its exclusive rights in Pittsburgh by bribes.[16] Public funds were left with favored depositories without interest, while the city borrowed from these same banks at a high rate of interest.[17] And down at the other end of the city vice stalked confidently before the eyes of police captains. Disorderly houses were managed by ward syndicates. The "promoter" would rent a house for $35 a month, for example, and rent it to prostitutes for $50 a week and protection. The tenants were required to buy their furniture from the official furniture man, their clothes from the "official wrapper maker," their beer from the "official bottler," and the prices were high. Such were the devices of the Magee-Flinn machine in Pittsburgh.[18]

New York's tale of fraud is no milder than the rest. The report of an investigating committee of the state legislature in 1876 revealed that the police and District Attorneys of New York City were organized in league with the gamblers and prostitutes to share in the plunder.[19] There were few trades or professions from which Tammany did not reap its share. Even the undertakers and coffin makers schemed for their business. Wyndon Lynn, an undertaker's assistant, testified before the Mazet Committee that James J. Warren had a monopoly on the dead bodies at Harlem Hospital. It was supposed to have been the duty of Harlem Hospital to notify the officials of the Bellevue Hospital in case of a death so that the latter could summon the relatives of the deceased. But Warren, a member of Tammany from that district, paid the clerk at Harlem Hospital to call him before Bellevue was notified. When the relatives arrived, the body was already in the care of the

---

[15] Steffens, *op. cit.*, pp. 147-149.
[16] *Ibid.*, pp. 149, 150.
[17] *Ibid.*, p. 165.
[18] *Ibid.*, pp., 165, 166.
[19] Nevins, *The Emergence of Modern America, 1865-1878*, p. 312.

undertaker.[20] Even pushcart peddlers and garbage and manure collectors paid high tribute to Tammany for their privileges.[21]

Much of the corruption in the administrative forces has rightly been blamed upon party prejudice. Intense partisanship so blinded the judgment of well-meaning citizens that dishonest tactics were winked at so long as the party was kept supreme. The politicians who dealt in local politics as a trade seized the opportunity and forged their machine zealously. They bound local and national issues together and, under the mask of party loyalty, proceeded to loot everything in sight. "Good men stolidly voted for and argued for the rottenest of local tickets rather than endanger their national party."[22] Even McKinley and Sherman urged that national issues be uppermost in the Cincinnati election of 1891, thus aiding in the victory of Horstmann, the candidate of Boss Cox.[23] The people were asked to vote for a Republican or a Democrat, not for policies of municipal administration.

Caucuses, conventions, and elections were all under party machine control. The Republican primary in Philadelphia, January 11, 1881, held for the purpose of choosing delegates for the nominating conventions on January 13, was a farce, so completely was it controlled by the bosses. The Mayoralty Convention, for example, with 199 delegates, received the following account in *Taggart's Sunday Times* on January 16, 1881: "An analysis of the personnel of the Convention which nominated Stokley will show that it was largely packed by office-holders and policemen. A summary of the occupations of the delegates shows that there were twenty-three policemen, four constables, nine members of city councils, five police magistrates, and eighty-six office-holders of one sort or another."[24]

Elections were fraudulent. Yet it was practically impossible to prosecute, for the judges were well paid by the machine. John Field, chairman of the Campaign Committee of Philadelphia's Committee of One Hundred, described to his associates how the employees of the gas trust were roused from their beds early on election morning, driven to the polls, and commanded to cast the ballots that were placed in their hands.[25] Bosses commonly im-

[20] Werner, *op. cit.*, pp. 431-433. The Mazet Committee made a lengthy report before the New York legislature in 1900 on public offices and municipal conditions in New York City.

[21] *Ibid.*, pp. 428, 429.

[22] Griffith, *op. cit.*, pp. 20, 21.

[23] *Ibid.*, p. 137.

[24] Vickers, *op. cit.*, pp. 123-128.

[25] *Ibid.*, p. 13.

ported large numbers of criminals and desperate characters, who, with the protection of the police and the election boards, intimidated and bullied voters. It is shocking to learn that most of these "foreign" desperadoes came from the offices of the Federal departments in the city of Washington![26] They were led in the seventies by one Russell, a native Philadelphian, whose earlier dishonesty in city politics had been rewarded by a profitable position with the national government. "He had acquired for himself a peculiar distinction as a leader of repeaters and ballot-box stuffers of the worst type, and no important election came on that he was not looked for anxiously by his political patrons who placed such a high value upon his services. . . . In many cases his acts alone frustrated the people's efforts and saved to the politicians important city offices."[27]

Party prejudices likewise controlled appointments to city offices. Through the spoils system the boss and his lieutenants hired their henchmen without any cost to themselves. The municipal salary list was little more than a fund to support corruption. During Stokley's three terms as Mayor of Philadelphia, up to 1880, he turned out of office 3,500 workers who failed in some way to do his bidding. And he required every municipal officeholder to pay $35 into the campaign fund for the election of 1880.[28]

Edward Bemis, in an article in *Public Opinion,* made this statement: "A recent chief of the Chicago Sanitary Department assured the writer that there were not six of his hundred subordinates whom he could trust. It was useless to dismiss anyone, for the chief must take in his place whomsoever some alderman may desire."[29] What hope, then, could the voters have had for efficiency or economy in the conduct of their city administration? In 1879, Boss McManes, as head of the Philadelphia gas trust, controlled 5,630 public jobs, which cost the city $3,877,316.82. The gas trustees, instead of receiving fixed salaries, were allowed to retain one-twelfth of the cost of appointments! Small wonder that McManes left an estate of more than $2,000,000.[30]

While blind party prejudice played havoc with elections and appointments, it also sought unfair advantage in the office of the tax collector. It was the custom to exempt officials and friends

---

[26] *Ibid.,* p. 57.
[27] *Ibid.,* p. 57.
[28] *Ibid.,* p. 12.
[29] Devlin, *Municipal Reform in the United States,* p. 86.
[30] Zink, Harold, *City Bosses in the United States: A Study of Twenty Municipal Bosses* (Durham, N. C., 1930), pp. 194-201.

of the party machine from the payment of taxes or from the penalties on delinquent taxes. The business of the tax office was conducted utterly without system; its accounts were always in a muddle. An investigation in Philadelphia in 1879 revealed that there were $9,795,149 in delinquent taxes owed to the city by officeholders and men of position, and that the Collector of Delinquent Taxes, authorized to retain 5% of his collections, had been keeping 11½%. In 1878 he had pocketed $147,500. The Common Council, apparently aroused more than usual, passed an act making it illegal for the Collector to keep more than 5%, but the Select Council voted it down, and the Governor, called upon for a veto, sustained the latter decision. Thus did the party machine legalize the stealing of taxes.[31]

"Safe are party bosses," wrote a political critic in 1883, "and with impunity may people's rights be abused, as long as they manage to have 'party lines' held superior to man's sense of right and justice. Wedded to party-prejudice men must become conscience-callous to the evils of their political organization, or they must divorce themselves therefrom, the last of which alternative requires courage."[32]

If this were all there were to the history of municipal government from 1875 to 1900, if there were nothing else to consider but growth and industrialization, weak charters, state interference, corrupt administration, it would be a woeful tale indeed. But courage was not entirely lacking. There were yet a few clear-minded men who pleaded for reform so persistently that the word passed from ear to ear, the scattered converts leagued together, and a great cry went up from embittered citizens. The battle for municipal reform was on!

---

[31] Allinson and Penrose, *Philadelphia 1681-1887: A History of Municipal Development.* pp. 234, 235.

[32] Vickers, *op. cit.*, p. 35.

CHAPTER THREE

Awakening Citizens

THOSE few energetic citizens who troubled themselves as early as 1875 to protest against the injustices of their cities were faced, first of all, by the problem of arousing public interest in the cause of reform. No reform, however local and limited its purpose, could be accomplished without the pressure of public opinion. People must be prodded into rebellion by having the story of municipal failure constantly dinned into their ears. Consequently, the movement, in its early years, was largely one of protest—protest against extravagance, graft, unfair appointments, poor sanitation, and all the many evils of the political machine. Wherever some specific abuse became so flagrant that it could no longer be endured in silence, there would gather together a few earnest citizens to register their disapproval and attempt to protect their rights. Occasionally they succeeded. Usually they failed because they could not command enough support to vitalize their efforts. Much of the work of reform was weak, misguided, unorganized. As a whole, it failed to strike at the fundamental causes of abuse, and was satisfied to attack some isolated problem, thereby making its achievements meager and temporary.

But there was still the encouraging memory of the overthrow of the Tweed Ring in 1871, and each new protest and constructive suggestion gave promise of increasing public interest. State legislatures were persuaded to appoint investigating committees to probe city affairs. Such alarming abuses were uncovered and proclaimed in the press and pulpit that municipal thought began gradually to crystallize around the problem of reform. It was promising to see political leaders giving time and thought to city government. Governor Tilden of New York and Governor Hantranft of Pennsylvania appointed commissions to study municipal affairs. In connection with the report of the New York commission in 1877, Tilden himself outlined the principles of home rule. That same year witnessed the gathering of a state municipal convention in Iowa for the discussion of mutual problems.[1] A few

---

[1] Griffith, *The Modern Development of City Government in the United Kingdom and in the United States*, vol. 1, p. 144.

states were sending official representatives to Europe to profit by the experiences of foreign cities.[2] Reform agitators in New York City made so bold as to organize a committee of 1,200 and put up a reform ticket in the election of 1878 in the hope of defeating Tammany.[3] The *New York Herald* took part in the fight by suggesting suitable candidates.[4] Boss Kelley, however, was too smart for them all; he proposed reform candidates of his own and bargained with the Republicans until the ticket was utterly confused and Tammany's success assured. But in spite of failure the committee was hailed as a brave and valuable experiment.

And so, by the persistence of a few, the talk of reform began to spread through the country and organizations were formed to take up the people's cause. Some were bent upon lowering taxes, others fought to dethrone corrupt officials while still others concerned themselves with civic betterment. Whatever their immediate purpose, all were pioneers in a cause that must have looked for many years like a losing battle.

Municipal reform in Philadelphia may be said to have started with the agitation against the Public Building Commission Act passed by the state legislature on August 5, 1870. The Act authorized the appointment of a board which could levy taxes for a public building program, and could spend the proceeds without being accountable to anyone. No term of years was designated for the services of the appointees; they had unlimited power to fill vacancies or to increase their number.[5] Some citizens became so aroused over the injustice of the Act that they called a mass meeting in the Acadamy of Music on March 24, 1871, and appointed a committee to support the bill for repeal which had already been introduced by Senator Robert P. Dechert.[6] All attempts at repeal failed, yet the incident so stirred popular feeling that a second mass meeting was called in June to consider the whole question of local mismanagement. A committee of two citizens from each ward was authorized to make up an independent ticket of reform

---

[2] Illinois, in 1872, and New Jersey, in 1877, sent education officials; Boston sent her Commissioner of Health in 1884. *Ibid.*, p. 143.

[3] *Nation*, vol. 27, July 11, 1878, p. 18.

[4] *Ibid.*, vol. 27, August 8, 1878, p. 75. Among the principal newspapers and magazines which rallied to the aid of reform were the *New York Herald*, the *New York Times*, the *Philadelphia Public Ledger*, the *Philadelphia Times*, the *North American Review*, the *Century*, the *Nation*, the *Chautauquan*, *McClure's Magazine*, the *Cosmopolitan*, and *Harper's Weekly*.

[5] Allinson and Penrose, *Philadelphia 1681-1887: A History of Municipal Development*, pp. 222-224; Vickers, *The Fall of Bossism, passim.*

[6] Vickers, *op. cit.*, Appendix, x, xi.

candidates for the coming election. In spite of opposition from both of the regular parties, the independents stubbornly conducted their canvass and were credited with 3,000 votes.[7]

The movement led to the organization of the Citizens' Municipal Reform Association on October 26, 1871, with Henry C. Lea as president.[8] Although non-partisan in purpose, the Association was composed almost entirely of Republicans. Pledging themselves to the improvement of the management of municipal affairs in general, the members of the association worked specifically for the substitution of fixed salaries for fees, the modification of registry and election laws (including the "slip-ticket" system), and changes in the State Constitution to limit the control of the legislature over the city.[9] They succeeded eventually in all three of their specific purposes and so cultivated public sentiment for reform that the field was well prepared for the formation of the Committee of One Hundred in 1880. It was the latter group which dealt decisive defeat to the candidates of Boss McManes in the election of February, 1881.[10]

The business men of Milwaukee entered the field of reform over the question of taxation. In 1875 the Wisconsin legislature permitted a tax levy of 17 mills, raised it in 1878, and in 1880 boosted it to 30 mills. The taxpayers became alarmed and under S. A. Harrison organized a Committee of One Hundred to fight the bill. They met with unforeseen success. In April, 1880, the legislature passed an act limiting the tax rate to 20 mills, except in cases of urgent necessity, when it might be raised to 25. The following year the city charter was amended, reducing the tax limit to 17½ mills.[11]

One of the first groups to adopt a broader program in the general interest of good government was the Citizens' Association of Chicago, organized on July 24, 1874, under Franklin Mac Veagh. Five objectives were outlined in the purpose of the Association:

---

[7] *Ibid.*, pp. 60, 61.

[8] The Citizens' Municipal Reform Association accomplished one of the rare victories of early reform in the Hart Creek Sewer contract case, when, by investigation of the actual cost of the work, it saved more than $20,000 of city funds. *Ibid.*, p. 18, Appendix, ii.

[9] *Ibid.*, p. 62.

[10] The Committee of One Hundred supported an independent ticket in the city election, February 15, 1881, with S. G. King, Democrat, for Mayor, and John Hunter, Republican, for Receiver of Taxes. King defeated Mayor Stokley by 6,000 votes, and Hunter had a majority of 20,000 over Pierie. *Ibid., passim.*

[11] Larson, Lawrence Marcellus, "A Financial and Administrative History of Milwaukee," Bulletin of the University of Wisconsin, No. 242, *Economic and Political Science Series*, vol. 4, 1908, pp. 124, 125.

to arouse interest in municipal legislation and administration, to promote projects for reform, to continue the investigation of the Police Department begun in 1873, to keep the public advised of civic problems, and to call attention to the needs of sanitation.[12] Similar to the Chicago group in its more inclusive purpose was the City Reform Club of New York City, started in 1879, and later identified with the Good Government Clubs.[13]

While some organizations concerned themselves primarily with questions of administration, others were formed in the interest of civic betterment. With the hard times following the Panic of 1873, cities were faced more than ever with problems of vice, poverty, public health, sweatshop abuses, and the like. In 1872 Anthony Comstock of New York City had raised his vehement protest against the circulation of obscene literature and in 1873 he became the founder of the Society for the Suppression of Vice. The object of the organization was a fight against vice, especially against the circulation of immoral literature. Mr. Comstock was among the few early crusaders who could show actual results for their labors.[14]

The year from 1873 to 1874 witnessed the remarkable Woman's Temperance Crusade in Ohio. This Crusade fought the liquor traffic so vigorously that in 50 days it cleaned 250 towns of the liquor business. From the nucleus of the movement came the founding of the Woman's Christian Temperance Union under Frances E. Willard in 1874.[15] In 1878, the Society for the Prevention of Crime was born in New York City. Its object was to remove the sources and causes of crime, to assist the weak in getting honest court protection, to urge the enforcement of liquor regulations, and to arouse public opinion in support of law and good citizenship. The work of this group developed so steadily that, with the aid of other reform agencies, it was able to muster forces strong enough to defeat Tammany Hall in the election of

---

[12] Tolman, William Howe, *Municipal Reform Movements in the United States* (New York, 1895), pp. 56, 57.

[13] *Ibid.*, p. 75.

[14] Comstock, Anthony, and others, "The Suppression of Vice," *North American Review*, vol. 135 (November, 1882), pp. 484-489. Anthony Comstock was born in Connecticut in 1844 and died in 1915. He was first inspired against the circulation of obscene literature by the Y. M. C. A. in 1868. In 1871 he offered his services to that organization in a crusade against vice. He formed a committee for the suppression of vice. In 1873 he became secretary of the society and served in this office the rest of his life. Van Doren, Mark, "Anthony Comstock," *Dictionary of American Biography*, vol. 4, pp. 330, 331.

[15] Schlesinger. Arthur M., *New Viewpoints in American History* (New York, 1922), pp. 151, 152.

November, 1894. The Society's exposure of police corruption was responsible for the later work of the Lexow Committee.[16]

Reform sentiment was aroused in New Orleans in 1894 as a result of the founding of the Auxiliary Sanitary Association, an organization designed to combat fraud and promote sanitation and good government. The Association's members appealed for private subscriptions for a fund to flush the gutters and accomplished their undertaking at a cost of $75,000; the city administration had fixed the cost for the same project at $200,000.[17]

And so, for one cause or another, groups like these were enlisting followers in all of the larger cities and adding strength to the first battle for reform, the arousal of public interest. During the period of the 1880's, however, reform forces suffered frequent reverses. With the return of prosperity and the improvement in state affairs, came recurring indifference toward city government. The fitful waves of reform were not always vigorous. Signs of progress were less frequent, less decisive. The forces of greed and unfair privilege took full advantage of the indifferent voters and strengthened their hold upon the political machine. Reform method, on the other hand, gave promise of improvement. It became not so much a matter of protest as one of corrective activity. Political reform was directed at more fundamental evils. Citizens' associations gave their first attention to the election of better city officials.

The experience of Philadelphia's Committee of One Hundred was an excellent example of the improvement in methods of reform.[18] When the Committee was organized through the efforts of Dunbar Lockwood on November 15, 1880, it was composed entirely of Republicans.[19] The nomination of proper Republican candidates for the election of February 15, 1881 was the major objective. The Committee outlined a Declaration of Principles and required that its candidates endorse it in writing. Among the points in the Committee's platform were the maintenance of a non-partisan police force, limitation of the compensation of the Receiver of Taxes, well paved and clean streets, a good water and

---

[16] Tolman, *op. cit.*, pp. 129, 130. The Lexow Committee was appointed by the state Senate to investigate the Police Department of New York City. The Committee delivered a five-volume report in 1895.

[17] Howe, William W., "Municipal History of New Orleans," Johns Hopkins University, *Studies in Historical and Political Science*, vol. 7 (April, 1889), p. 185.

[18] *Ante*, p. 27.

[19] John Wanamaker presented the first resolution at the opening meeting of the Committee of One Hundred. Vickers, *op. cit.*, p. 88.

gas supply at a lower cost, non-partisan election of the school board, appointment of teachers solely on merit, and prosecution and punishment of those guilty of election fraud, maladministration of office, or misappropriation of public funds.[20] The Committee nominated Mayor W. S. Stokley as its candidate for re-election and John Hunter for Receiver of Taxes.

Stokley, to the astonishment of the reformers, refused to sign the Committee's Declaration of Principles, thereby casting his lot with the Republican machine of Boss McManes. Aroused by the Mayor's refusal of their support, the Committee of One Hundred realized that party lines were not broad enough for reform, that machine control could be broken only through "the joint efforts of Republicans and Democrats, acting as citizens and not as partisans."[21] During the same meeting at which the Committee withdrew its nomination of Stokley there was adopted a resolution to revise the Declaration of Principles on non-partisan lines and invite the co-operation of a committee of Democrats. As a result, the reform element of the Democratic Party joined forces with the Committee. The coalition supported S. G. King, Democrat, for Mayor, and John Hunter, Republican, for Receiver of Taxes. Both reform candidates were victorious.[22] This signal victory of Philadelphia's Committee of One Hundred offered an encouraging example of the increasing tendency toward bi-partisanship in civic reform.[23]

Other citizens' organizations throughout the country were likewise bending particular effort to the endorsement of suitable candidates for election. The Citizens' Association of Albany, founded in 1881, was non-partisan and hired a special attorney to assist in uncovering fraud in the city and county administrations.[24] In Baltimore public sentiment was stirred over the exposure of fraudulent elections in 1875 and 1885. In November, 1885, a group of Baltimore citizens organized the Reform League, establishing clubs in each ward for the purpose of recommending good candidates and securing fair elections. Through this agency the voters of Baltimore secured the Australian ballot.[25] In Cincinnati the

---

[20] *Ibid.*, pp. 111-114.
[21] *Ibid.*, Appendix, xxv, xxvi.
[22] *Ibid.*, p. 231; *ante*, p. 27. The Young Men's Democratic Association and the American Club, a Democratic organization, met and endorsed Hunter. *Ibid.*, pp. 163-166.
[23] The ring was not definitely defeated until 1887 when Boss McManes was permanently deprived of his position with the gas trust.
[24] Tolman, *op. cit.*, pp. 51, 52.
[25] *Ibid.*, pp. 124-128.

Committee of One Hundred, founded in 1885, and its successor, the Citizens' Club, founded in 1893, emphasized the need of election and police reform and prosecuted and convicted ten men, some of them prominent officials, for fraud in elections and administration.[26] New Orleans also had a Committee of One Hundred, organized in 1885, whose major purpose was to publish the records of Councilmen and to fight for the repeal of such Council legislation as they deemed illegal or injurious.[27] Working with this Committee was the Young Men's Democratic Association, founded in October, 1887, the members of which guarded the polls on election day, April 17, 1888.[28]

There were many other similar groups: the Citizens' Municipal Association of Philadelphia (organized on April 20, 1886), which forced the streetcar company to pave the streets they had damaged and recovered several hundred thousand dollars owed to the city by that company; the Citizens' Association of Boston (founded on December 27, 1887), which defeated undesirable rapid transit measures and lowered the rates for electric light service; the Massachusetts Society for Promoting Good Citizenship (started in Boston in December, 1887), which promoted good laws and lectures on citizenship; and the Library Hall Association of Cambridge, Massachusetts (founded December 18, 1889), which was principally concerned with the endorsement of qualified candidates. In 1893 the Library Hall Association endorsed eleven Alderman, of whom nine were elected; twenty Common Councilmen, of whom eighteen were successful; and five school committeemen, all elected.[29]

There were indications during this period of the tendency toward centralization of reform agencies. Local units were banding together into state and national organizations. Representatives of the Law and Order Leagues of eight states met in Boston on December 22, 1883, and founded the International Law and Order League to promote education in citizenship.[30] The American Institute of Civics, with branches in all the large cities, was organized in Boston in 1885. The national unit of the latter organization sponsored the publication of the *American Magazine of Civics*.[31] The National Civil Service Reform League incorporated 31 local

[26] *Ibid.*, pp. 58, 59.
[27] Howe, "Municipal History of New Orleans," p. 186.
[28] *Ibid.*, p. 187.
[29] Tolman, *op. cit.*, pp. 53, 54, 64, 65, 101-104.
[30] *Ibid.*, pp. 100, 101.
[31] *Ibid.*, pp. 48, 49.

units in 1881 and began the publication of the magazine, *Good Government*. In 1893 the National Civil Service Reform League had 10,000 members.[32] In 1881 the Charity Organization Society of the City of New York began its work of unifying existing charity groups and encouraging closer relationship in state and municipal charities.[33]

In spite of the increase in the number and scope of reform agencies during the eighties and the partial arousal of public interest, the movement had not yet become a dynamic force in municipal development. There were countless hindrances to its effectiveness, as the mass of the people were only too ready to discover. To the average ear there was something distasteful about the word "reform." It suggested denunciation, fault-finding, prudishness. Because many professional reformers were incompetent and untrained, the group as a whole came to be looked upon generally as cranks and theorists.[34] Many of the mass meetings offered nothing more than empty speeches, wordy harangues that failed to define specific issues or to advance sound solutions. While the party in office made a cunning attempt to win votes by proposing definite improvements, the reform party merely played the role of critic. Denunciation did not solve the problem; popular indignation was too unsteady a fire. "The attitude of criticism is a primary source of reform weakness and instability," declared a scholar of the period.[35]

Moreover, many reformers were so determined to accomplish their own particular ends that they were blinded to the greater good and unwilling to concede and cooperate. One group wanted to clear the city of vice, another wanted lower taxes; each blamed its failure upon the selfishness of the other. The banner of reform was frequently dragged into arguments that were nothing more than factional fights.[36]

A third difficulty arose when politicians discovered that, by adopting a reform program of their own, they could float into office on the crest of popular sentiment. When the enthusiasm of reform died down, they were free to proceed as they chose. Ed-

---

[32] *Ibid.*, pp. 121, 122.
[33] *Ibid.*, pp. 145, 146.
[34] Mowry, Duane, "Reform and Reformers," *American Magazine of Civics*, vol. 7 (November, 1895), pp. 462-464.
[35] Young, James T., "The Basis of Present Reform Movements," American Academy of Political and Social Science, *Annals*, vol. 29 (March, 1903). pp. 244, 245.
[36] Werner. *Tammany Hall*, pp. 444, 445.

ward Cooper was elected Mayor of New York in 1878 on the reform platform of anti-Tammany and Republican forces. The *New York Times* prophesied a great reform program under the new Mayor. But once in office, Cooper was none too scrupulous about his conduct. When it was discovered that he had bargained with Aldermen for appointments for certain of his friends, the people were indignant. The *Nation* magazine published a bitter indictment of Cooper, accusing him of intriguing and dickering with the bosses, failing to carry out the program for which he had been elected. "The way to get reform is to fight," declared the *Nation's* editors.[37]

Another hindrance to the progress of reform was the fact that the public was inclined to be skeptical, fickle, and easily discouraged. Whipped up by the excitement of a political campaign, the average man expected to see immediate changes. The few genuine reformers who were elected to office usually found the system so honeycombed with corruption that their efforts were futile. The people then became impatient and shifted their loyalty to another man or another cause.[38] One of the greatest deficiencies of the early reform movement was this failure of the citizens as a whole to offer steady, voluntary support, an asset that could not be obtained by laws or constitutions.[39]

---

[37] "Municipal and Federal Reform," *Nation*, vol. 31 (December 30, 1880), pp. 454-456.

[38] Devlin, *Municipal Reform in the United States*, pp. 9-13.

[39] MacVeagh, Franklin, "A Programme of Municipal Reform," *American Journal of Sociology*, vol. 1 (March, 1896), p. 552. In New York City, on election night in 1897, when returns showed that Tammany was again victorious in spite of the efforts of reformers, people paraded the streets, yelling "Well, well, reform has gone to Hell." Many carried cardboards bearing the words, "I told you so." Werner, *op. cit.*, p. 457.

CHAPTER FOUR

The Great Era of Reform

THE era from 1890 to 1900 may rightly be called the great era of reform. Dissatisfied with the meager achievements of earlier years, earnest citizens began to study the weaknesses of reform and to search for fundamental solutions of municipal problems. They centered their attention upon definite issues, especially those issues involving big business and state interference. They spent less time in rebellion and protest, more time in analytical research.

The wave of public interest was climaxed by the founding of the National Municipal League, which grew out of the first National Conference for Good City Government. Launched in Philadelphia in January, 1894, the Conference was held at the suggestion of Herbert Welsh of the Municipal League of Philadelphia. Representatives to the Conference came from New York, Brooklyn, Chicago, Boston, Baltimore, Minneapolis, Milwaukee, Albany, Buffalo, Columbus, and Philadelphia.[1] They studied and compared their mutual problems and advocated civil service reform and separate city elections.[2] As a direct outgrowth of this meeting came the organization, in May, 1894, of the National Municipal League with 16 affiliated local units. By 1895 there were 180 branch leagues, and in 1896, 80 or 90 more local groups were founded. The most vigorous organizations were in the Middle Atlantic states, where municipal government was at its worst and the problems most complex. New York and New Jersey alone had 56 such societies. In 1897 the National Municipal League appointed a committee to draft a model city charter. The following year the charter was adopted as a distinct feature of the League's reform program, embodying, as it did, the principles of home rule, government by experts, fixed responsibility, simplification of municipal frameworks, and published accounts of city finances.[3]

The founding of the National Municipal League offered

---

[1] Welsh, Herbert, "A Definite Step Towards Municipal Reform," *Forum*, vol. 17 (April, 1894), pp. 179-182. The New Orleans delegation missed railroad connections and failed to arrive in time for the meeting.

[2] *Ibid.*, pp. 182-185.

[3] Faulkner, *Quest for Social Justice*, p. 99.

evidence of the tremendous stimulus that had come to the whole reform movement. Interest was high throughout the country. Hundreds of new groups were being organized, some to promote the general interests of a good citizenship program, others with special projects to pursue. Among the most active civic clubs were the Municipal League of Philadelphia (founded in 1892), the City Government Club of Pittsburgh (1893), the Committee of Fifty of Albany (1893), the Good Government Clubs of New York City (1893), the Municipal Club of Rochester (1894), the Municipal League of Boston (1894), the Citizens' Protective Association of New Orleans (1894), the Committee of Public Safety of St. Louis (1894), the Civic Federation of Detroit (1894), and the Civic Federation of Chicago (1895).[4]

The Municipal League of Milwaukee, founded in March, 1893, stated among its primary purposes the elimination of state and national issues from local politics and the promotion of civil service reform.[5] The Citizens' Federation of Toledo was organized in October, 1894, by the chairmen of the Pastors' Union and the Christian Endeavor County Union; this Federation enlisted in its membership some of the strongest business men and lawyers of the city and took an active part in law enforcement regarding gambling, saloons, Sunday desecration, and disorderly houses.[6] The Municipal League of Pittsburgh was launched at a mass meeting in 1895 for the specific purpose of defeating the political machine in the election of February, 1896. The League nominated G. W. Guthrie for Mayor on an independent ticket and lost by only a narrow margin. In attempting to secure voluntary contributions, the League met frequent refusals from business men who withheld support on the grounds that it was easier for them to do business with one boss than with the whole people.[7] The Good Government Clubs of Baltimore, with the support of the press, scored a victory against the Gorman-Rasin ring in the elections of 1895.[8]

New York City witnessed a dramatic reform movement when in 1891 Dr. Charles H. Parkhurst, pastor of the Madison Square

---

[4] Tolman, *Municipal Reform Movements in the United States, passim;* Woodruff, Clinton Rogers, "The Progress of Municipal Reform," *Municipal Affairs,* vol. 1 (June, 1897), pp. 303-308; Steffens, *The Shame of the Cities,* pp. 223-242.

[5] Tolman, *op. cit.,* pp. 112, 113.

[6] *Ibid.,* pp. 59, 60.

[7] Steffens, *op. cit.,* pp. 178-180.

[8] Howard, C. M., "The Recent Revolt in Baltimore: Its Results and Lessons," National Conference for Good City Government, *Proceedings for 1896,* pp. 75-85.

Church, became president of the Society for the Prevention of Crime.[9] Dr. Parkhurst visited New York's underworld in disguise and collected positive evidence to prove his contention that Tammany Hall protected and instigated vice for its own profit. The exposures he proclaimed from his pulpit attracted wide attention. Twice he was called before a Grand Jury for statements he had made against city officials and the Police Department. On January 25, 1894, the local Chamber of Commerce passed a resolution asking for a legislative investigation of New York's police system. The result was the Lexow Committee of the State Senate. That Committee's exhaustive report in 1895 exerted a lasting influence in the cause of reform.[10]

In Cleveland the Chamber of Commerce entered the fight for civic reform in 1892. It began by arousing the indignation of the people against the administration's neglect of harbor conditions, public grounds, roads, and sanitation. In the election of 1895 it was largely responsible for the success of men who stood for an extensive civic program. The City Council called in members of the Chamber of Commerce for advice in questions of municipal improvements.[11]

The work of religious organizations in this new wave of municipal reform is well illustrated by the active citizenship campaign sponsored by the Christian Endeavor Societies of the Presbyterian Church. At the twelfth International Christian Endeavor Convention in Montreal in 1893 the president, Francis E. Clark, urged the societies to line up with their local reform forces, to stand for good men and good laws, and to oppose vigorously saloons, gambling dens, lotteries, and Sabbath violations.[12] In 1894 an affiliated society in Wisconsin urged the people of Madison and Janesville to attend the polls and presented a petition to the state legislature recommending a Corrupt Practice Act. A Christian Endeavor Society supported a reform ticket in Walla Walla, Washington, in 1894, and brought about the closing of saloons on Sunday. In Orlando, Florida, the local society campaigned to get voters to pledge attendance at the primaries. At Shenandoah, Iowa, some

---

[9] *Ante*, pp. 28, 29.

[10] Parkhurst, Dr. Charles H., *My Forty Years in New York* (New York, 1923), pp. 106-141; Werner, *Tammany Hall*, pp. 348-355.

[11] Ritchie, Ryerson, "Commercial Organizations and Municipal Reform," National Conference for Good City Government, *Proceedings for 1897*, pp. 120-124.

[12] Baer, John Willis, "The Work of Christian Endeavor Societies in Behalf of Better Citizenship," National Conference for Good City Government, *Proceedings for 1895*, pp. 517-523.

young churchgoers supported a bill to prohibit the sale of tobacco to minors. In Illinois the Humphrey Bill, a measure in the interest of race track gambling, passed in the Senate but was defeated in the House, partly because of the flood of petitions and letters from Christian Endeavor Societies all over the state. The societies in Syracuse, New York, set out to fight for the closing of slot machines and gambling houses; within one month the Mayor had suppressed the machines and the judges were convicting gamblers. In this same city 68 saloon keepers prevailed upon the City Council to forbid temperance night lunch wagons but when the Christian Endeavor Society demanded that the law be repealed and presented a petition with 3,000 names, it was hastily scratched off the books.[13]

At Camden, New Jersey, the Baptist Young People's Unions, the Christian Endeavor Societies, and the Epworth Leagues joined forces and organized a Christian Citizenship Union in 1895. They enlisted in their ranks 2,000 voters and many more young people. It was their purpose to acquaint themselves with municipal government, expose the neglect of city affairs, oppose vice, and urge better government.[14]

All of the reform agencies mentioned are but examples of many others that actively joined the struggle during the last decade of the century. From the business world, from professional life, from the church came volunteers to promote their mutual interests.

Even from the home came women with energetic and enthusiastic support. While most of the civic clubs had not restricted their membership to men, it was not until the 1890's that they began to invite the active co-operation of the women, as did the Civic Federation of Chicago.[15] Civic organizations exclusively for women became more prominent. The National Women's Health Protective Association had branches in many large cities and worked for the promotion of public health and the enforcement of sanitation laws.[16] The Municipal Order League of Chicago, founded in 1892, employed an inspector to assemble information on city conditions and keep the public informed of the most pressing needs. It succeeded in securing an appropriation for the construction of the first free public bath and for the opening of drinking

---

[13] *Ibid.*, pp. 519-521.
[14] Lawson, Albert G., "A Christian Citizenship League," *National Conference for Good City Government, Proceedings for 1896*, p. 275.
[15] Tolman, *op. cit.*, p. 167.
[16] *Ibid., passim.*

fountains throughout the city.[17] In Brooklyn the Civitas Club, organized in 1893, exerted so great an influence in arousing public interest that it was one of the strongest forces in the overthrow of the political ring through the election of Mayor Schieren that year.[18]

By the dawn of the twentieth century the battle for municipal reform was in full swing. It had slowly gathered strength, developing from the weak and fitful protests of a few into the organized and disciplined attack of thousands of citizens. The year 1900 witnessed frequent official investigations in the large cities. America was staying home to clean house. The first victory was won; the people were aroused to their civic responsiblities.

How thoroughly the reformers succeeded in cleaning house during those 25 years, to what extent they met and solved the evils of the municipal system is quite another question. The most obvious and pressing aspects of the struggle were in the fight against corruption. With the exposure of graft, fraud, and inefficiency the natural reaction of the public was to change the personnel of local governments and get rid of the professional politicians. Too often, however, most citizens failed to see that by removing individuals they were not improving city administration or striking at its fundamental weaknesses. This would have to come later. For the present, popular attention was largely centered upon the more tangible problem of the political machine and its glaring injustice.

There were various methods of attack in the battle for better city government. The fight usually began with investigations and criticisms of the administration in power, attempts to prosecute corrupt officials in the courts, agitation for police reform. When election time approached, it was customary for the reform forces to study the records of party candidates and endorse those who best satisfied their demands. Where reform agencies were comparatively strong, they would sometimes attempt to contest the election with an independent party and a separate slate of reform candidates. The third party, however, was neither permanently nor usually successful.

The civic clubs of New York City bent every effort during the nineties to defeat Tammany Hall once and for all. The public was so aroused over the reports of lawlessness and the power of Tammany under Richard Croker that determination to fight him

[17] *Ibid.*, pp. 171-173.
[18] *Ibid.*, pp. 167-170.

in the election of 1894 became considerable. The Good Government Clubs, the Citizens' Union, the Society for the Prevention of Crime, the Citizens' Association, and the City Club all had committees at work on election plans. During the summer a movement was started to fuse all of these organizations into one powerful group. It was not an easy task; each wanted its own program to be uppermost and for a while union seemed impossible. However, a united front meeting was finally held at Cooper Union and William L. Strong, a bank president and a man of the highest reputation, nominated as the reform candidate for Mayor. When the election returns came in, Strong had defeated the Tammany candidate.[19] Theodore Roosevelt was one of the ardent supporters of the concerted action of the reform units in fighting corrupt administration. Roosevelt was later appointed Police Commissioner under Mayor Strong and effected a temporary scouring of the Police Department.[20]

But the victory in the office of Mayor could not break the strong wall of the machine. The report of the Lexow Committee in 1895 on its investigation of the Police Department came as a distinct shock. John W. Goff, counsel for the Committee, uncovered a mass of evidence showing Tammany's firm grip on the city and the utter corruption of the police force. Saloon keepers, prostitutes, and gamblers had confessed before the Committee that they paid huge sums of money for police and court protection. Police Commissioner James J. Martin had testified that between 85% and 90% of the appointments, promotions, and transfers in his department had been made upon the recommendations of Tammany leaders in the districts in question.[21] The People's Municipal League discovered that when it had collected funds in 1890 to oppose Tammany, the same firms that had made contributions to satisfy their moral obligations had contributed likewise to Tammany to insure their safety after the election.[22]

As the evidence of corruption increased with each new investigation, interest focused upon the election of 1897. The Republicans, hoping to stay in power, endorsed B. F. Tracy for Mayor on a straight Republican ticket. The reform candidate was Seth Low, Mayor of Brooklyn from 1882 to 1886 and a former presi-

---

[19] Werner, op. cit., pp. 442-443.
[20] Bishop, Joseph Bucklin, Theodore Roosevelt and His Time Shown in His Own Letters (New York, 1920), vol. 1, pp. 59-62.
[21] Werner, op. cit., pp. 356-379.
[22] "Responsibility for Political Corruption," Century, vol. 44 (July, 1892), p. 474.

dent of Columbia University. Tammany Hall did not announce
its candidate until a few weeks before the election. It had waited
for the return of Boss Croker. Robert A. Van Wyck, a city judge,
was selected the night before the official Democratic nominating
convention assembled. Civic organizations fought desperately
for Seth Low, hoping to repeat their former success. But Van
Wyck won by a plurality of 85,000. Tammany was restored to
complete power for four more years and New York City reached
the new century still waging battle against a corrupt administration.[23]

Unlike New York, Chicago faced the year 1900 with at least
one definite victory to her credit. Slowly but consistently the
reform party had won a majority in the City Council. In 1895 the
Municipal Voters' League had been founded, a non-partisan organization with a platform of municipal reform. The League appointed a Committee of Nine, with George E. Cole as chairman,
to investigate the records of political candidates and endorse or
reject them as their records justified. It happened that the Municipal Voters' League came into existence when the Chicago City
Council was at its worst. Although there was plenty of police
graft and administrative abuse in Chicago, the Council was the
heart of corruption. Two-thirds of the Councilmen were organized
into a bi-partisan combination, with big business behind them, to
put over the deals in public contracts—the chief source of Chicago's graft. So George Cole and his associates struck at the Council
with all their force. In 1895 the Committee of Nine branded as
"thieves" 57 of the 68 Aldermen. Of the 34 Aldermen whose terms
would expire at the coming election, the League refused to endorse
all but eight. The Committee studied each ward and published
accounts of its findings. It distributed circulars, conducted a house-
to-house canvass, held mass meetings and parades. As the result
of its fight only ten of the undesirable Aldermen were renominated
and only six finally elected.[24] With each election the Municipal
Voters' League kept hammering at the Council, gradually strengthening its hold until in 1899 it won a clear majority. By 1900 the
reform element controlled two-thirds of the Council. This success
was one of the most promising victories in the fight for honest
city officials.[25]

---

[23] Werner, *op. cit.*, pp. 450-456. In 1897 the legislature passed an act
creating Greater New York and increasing the Mayor's term of office to four
years. *Ibid.*, p. 451.
    [24] Steffens, *op. cit.*, pp. 242-248.
    [25] *Ibid.*, pp. 256-259.

While Chicago reformers were cleaning up the City Council, St. Louis was just beginning to observe the sensational exposure of an administration that for years had enjoyed an astonishing profit in graft. Since 1882 St. Louis had groaned under the iron hand of Ed Butler. A blacksmith by trade, Boss Butler began his political career in 1876, when he was paid to deliver votes against the new charter. By clever scheming he rose, step by step, to the control of the Republican machine in St. Louis. Some of the newspapers had been protesting for a long time against municipal corruption and the citizens' reform agencies objected in vain. The difficulty lay in the fact that back of the corruption stood wealthy men, respected in business and in church, who felt obliged to support the machine from which they obtained privileges.[26] With the approach of the election of 1900, Democratic Party leaders decided to take added precaution and attract votes by raising the cry of "reform." The Independents agreed with the Democrats to put up a ticket of irreproachable candidates, ignoring national issues, and declaring themselves exclusively for good government.[27] Party leaders, of course, had no intention of carrying out their program or giving up their loot.

One of the candidates on the fake reform ticket was Joseph W. Folk, who had consented to run for the office of Circuit Attorney. When the party leaders first interviewed Folk and asked him to appear on the ticket, he warned them that he would prosecute the lawless element and fulfill the duties of the office. They heartily agreed with him, assuring themselves silently that this was just a conventional promise and that he would be easy to manage. The entire "reform" slate was victorious and Joseph W. Folk, three weeks after taking the oath of office, began a most startling exposure of the corruption that had festered St. Louis for so many years.[28]

Folk received his first clues about the true state of affairs in St. Louis from James M. Galvin, who had gathered the threads of gossip and published them.[29] The new Circuit Attorney set vigorously to work and sent his lieutenants out gathering information on the municipal corruption of the past ten years. He revealed such alarming facts on election frauds and bribery that wealthy men found it convenient to leave the city on extended business tours.

---

[26] *Ibid.*, pp. 36, 37.
[27] Blair, James L., "The St. Louis Disclosures," National Conference for Good City Government, *Proceedings for 1903*, p. 96.
[28] Steffens, *op. cit.*, pp. 37-39.
[29] Blair, *loc. cit.*, p. 92.

The blackest years were found to be 1898, 1899, and 1900—a period under the Republican administration of Mayor Ziegenheim. "Foreign" corporations had come in and driven out home industries. Both political parties were guilty of the most daring fraud. Franchises worth millions were granted without one cent of cash to the city and only small future payments. Payrolls were padded beyond recognition.[30]

The Council, although utterly illiterate, had an elaborate system of fees governing all votes. No franchise was granted without a specified fee for each of the Councilmen. There was a regular price required for a vote on a grain elevator privilege, another price for a street improvement job. In cases of strong opposition, the fees were higher. One Councilman swore before a Grand Jury that he received $50,000 for his vote on a certain measure.[31]

The details of Folk's probe were appalling. In the Central Traction deal the street railway franchise had been sold by the Council for $250,000 in bribes, but with no profit to the city. Robert M. Snyder, who bought the franchise, sold it again for $1,250,000.[32] A lighting bill had been bribed through the House of Delegates for $47,500.[33] In the Garbage Contract deal the privilege of collecting garbage had been secured for $200,000 by bribery of the Board of Health.[34] It was reported that one of the "innocent" Councilmen consulted a lawyer about bringing suit against a corporation that had failed to pay his voting fee. Supplies for public institutions found their way, by prearrangement, to the homes of party leaders. One account listed imported cheese and French wines as food for the poorhouse.[35]

The result of Folk's investigation was a series of prosecutions and convictions. He brought Charles H. Turner, president of the Suburban Railroad Company, and P. H. Stock, secretary of the St. Louis Brewing Company, before the Grand Jury and there secured evidence of a $114,000 bribery that led to the conviction of C. H. Kelley, C. J. Denney, and H. A. Faulkner of the Council.[36] In the spring of 1901, a genuine reform Mayor was elected. In

---

[30] Steffens, *op. cit.*, pp. 35, 36.
[31] *Ibid.*, pp. 33-35.
[32] Fowler, B. O., "Twenty-Five Years of Bribery and Corrupt Practices," *Arena*, vol. 31 (January, 1904), pp. 28, 29; Blair, *loc. cit.*, pp. 87, 88.
[33] Fowler, *loc. cit.*, p. 29.
[34] Blair, *loc. cit.*, p. 88.
[35] Steffens, *op. cit.*, pp. 33-35.
[36] *Ibid.*, p. 104.

1902 and 1903 the fight against corruption reached its climax and St. Louis was, for a time at least, "cleaned up."[37]

During these same years the citizens of many other cities were engaged in similar efforts to free themselves of machine rule, oust the dishonest and inefficient personnel of their administrations, and improve their government in general. In 1890 Boston and Providence had both elected reform Mayors.[38] Toledo and Detroit witnessed a successful fight to replace professional politicians by candidates endorsed by the civic leagues.

---

[37] Blair, *loc. cit.*, p. 96.

[38] "Organized Municipal Reform," *Century*, vol. 41 (March, 1891), pp. 789, 790.

CHAPTER FIVE

Toward Better Government

IN addition to the removal and exposure of corrupt officials, there were a score of other problems during the years 1875-1900. There was the task of trying to get a fair proportion of the qualified voters out to the polls. There was the essential matter of improving the methods of voting by laws governing primaries, fraud and separate elections. There was the urgent need for court reforms. There were the evils of the spoils system and the influences of monopoly and big business. There were vexing problems of municipal finance. The road ahead was by no means straight or smooth.

Reform organizations spent a large part of their time urging citizens to exercise their rights of franchise—but with little success. In 24 of the largest cities an average of 50% of the qualified voters cast their ballots in the elections of 1896. The stay-at-homers in Pennsylvania increased from 70,000 in 1888 to 610,000 in 1895; in New York from 75,000 to 510,000; in Massachusetts from 80,000 to 230,000; in Ohio from 40,000 to 180,000. In one election in Georgia in 1896 only nine per cent of the voters appeared at the polls.[1] There were some who advocated a limitation of the franchise so that the taxpayers, who carried the expense of government, would have a greater proportion of the votes. In 1886 only one-fifth of the voters in Boston were taxpayers.[2] The questions of proper representation at the polls, however, remained largely unsolved.

Some little progress was made in the effort to regulate the primaries and insure equal rights. By 1897 more than half of the states had laws controlling primaries, but their regulations failed to secure justice.[3] Between 1882 and 1904 the New York legislature passed 21 laws for primaries, but the nominations were still autocratic, controlled neither by a majority nor even by a plural-

---

[1] Pomeroy, Eltweed, "The Doorway of Reform," *Arena*, vol. 17 (April, 1897), p. 713.

[2] Browne, George Morgan, "Municipal Reform," *New Englander*, vol. 45 (February, 1886), pp. 152, 153.

[3] Insley, Edward, "How to Reform the Primary-Election System," *Arena*, vol. 17 (June, 1897), p. 1016.

ity.[4] Only Kentucky and Missouri really supervised the primaries and attempted to aid. Kentucky, by a law passed in 1879, had direct primary nominations and no conventions.[5] The Chicago Civic Federation presented a reformed primary law to the Illinois legislature in 1897. Its members went to Springfield in a body to urge the passage of a law requiring separate primary elections for each party and on different days. The original provisions were so modified by the time the bill passed the legislature that the Federation considered its attempt at primary reform a complete failure.[6]

The fight for the separation of city elections from state and national elections showed better results, although it was not until after 1890 that the idea gained much headway. Thinking people were becoming convinced that the dissociation of local and national issues would help to focus the attention of the voters upon purely municipal questions. "Golden Rule" Jones, Mayor of Toledo from 1897 to 1904, fought hard for the principle of non-partisanship in local government. He called himself "A Man Without a Party."[7] Naturally, the politicians, needing party issues to carry them into office, put up a vigorous oppostion on the ground that a separate city election would cost too much. Boston and Providence were both successful in securing separate elections and the victories of the reform tickets in those two cities in 1890 were believed due to the fact that the municipal elections were held independent of state and national.[8]

However important primary regulations and separate elections may have been, reformers mustered far greater strength in the battle against fraudulent elections. Party machines had become so bold in practices of intimidation and fraud that public sentiment was quickly aroused against them. Members of municipal leagues frequently guarded the polls to watch for ballot-box stuffers and bring them to prosecution.

Philadelphia was awakened to the injustice of her elections in February, 1880, when William Conway, the taxpapers' candi-

---

[4] Deming, Horace E., "Municipal Nomination Reforms," American Academy of Political and Social Science, *Annals,* vol. 25 (March, 1905), pp. 204, 205.

[5] Insley, *loc. cit.,* p. 1017.

[6] *Ibid.,* pp. 1020, 1021.

[7] Whitlock, Brand, *Forty Years of It* (New York, 1914), pp. 138, 139. Samuel M. Jones, Mayor of Toledo from 1897 to 1904, was one of the outstanding mayors of his generation. He sought to conduct the city government on the basis of the Golden Rule. *Ibid.,* pp. 114, 115; Faulkner, *Quest for Social Justice* p. 94.

[8] "Organized Municipal Reform," *Century,* vol. 41 (March, 1891), pp. 789, 790.

date for Common Council, saw a professional repeater casting fraudulent votes atı the Fifth Ward polling place. When Conway requested the police to arrest the offender, he was himself attacked and hustled out into the street. Indignant at such treatment, he went straight to the office of Mayor Stokley to protest, but the Mayor only remarked, "Would not your party do the same thing if they had the power?" Conway's opponent won by a majority of 100, but the election was contested in court for 18 months and so many illegal practices were exposed that the eyes of the public were opened at last.[9] The Committee of One Hundred voted to exert every effort to protect the citizens at the following election in February, 1881.

Two days before the hotly-contested election, two of the Philadelphia papers, *Taggart's Sunday Times* and the *Sunday Mercury*, reported that this would be the most corrupt in the history of the city. Boss McManes had collected an election fund of $200,000, $170,000 coming from corporations and $30,000 from officeholders (the latter were required to pay individual assessments as high as $50).[10] The Committee of One Hundred redoubled their precautions. They offered a ten-dollar reward for the detection of any election officer who violated the law, and a five-dollar reward for evidence of illegal voting. They secured a promise from District Attorney Graham that all violators would be prosecuted to the full extent of the law. Then they distributed circulars throughout the city pledging themselves to the protection of the ballot.[11] The work of the reformers was well repaid. It was in this election that the reform candidates, King and Hunter, were placed in the offices of Mayor and Receiver of Taxes.[12]

In the Baltimore mayoralty election of 1885 the Independent Democratic nominee, a life-long member of the Democratic Party and a man of unimpeachable character, was endorsed by the Republicans as a reform candidate. The Democratic machine nominated an outspoken politician who frankly supported machine rule. On the face of the election returns the regular Democratic candidate won by an insignificant majority. The reform forces, however, discovered and published proof of election fraud, and the election judges were convicted. In order to secure fair elections

[9] Vickers, *The Fall of Bossism*, pp. 3-7.
[10] *Ibid.*, p. 224.
[11] *Ibid.*, pp. 215, 216.
[12] *Ante*, p. 30.

and punish violators the Reform League was immediately organized to protect the voters' rights in Baltimore.[13]

There were similar efforts being made in other cities as fraudulent elections were revealed. In New Orleans in 1887 and 1888 the Committee of One Hundred cleared from the registration books 12,000 names that had been placed there by fraud.[14] Alabama passed a law in 1893 requiring each voter to furnish a certificate of registration before receiving a ballot and to surrender the certificate when his vote had been cast.[15] The citizens of Albany organized a Committee of Fifty in 1893, after the exposure of fraud in their November elections, and this committee assisted in the prosecution of the fraudulent forces. Although several arrests were made, the ring so intimidated the jury that there were no convictions. But for the charter election of 1894 the reformers organized an Honest Election Party and successfully guarded the polls.[16] By such efforts as these local reform agencies exerted a definite influence toward the improvement of methods and regulations in municipal elections.

Another question of city administration which attracted the attention of a few of the municipal leagues was the matter of court reforms. The Citizens' League of Camden, New Jersey, was organized in October, 1893, to oppose the Gloucester race track. The track had become a vicious influence in political circles, for its owners sought to defend their business by dictating election nominations and controlling city boards. The worst obstacle in the way of law and order was the fact that the courts were tampered with and the juries "fixed" for the protection of the race track owners and their patrons. The Citizens' League tackled the difficult problem and claimed at least temporary success.[17]

The Civic Federation of Detroit fought vigorously to combat law court conditions. It forced a bill through the legislature in 1895 raising the qualifications of jurors, requiring the judges to see that the jurors were properly qualified, and speeding up trials in the municipal courts.[18] In the same year in New York City reform sentiment triumphed by requiring a complete reorganization in city judicial affairs. The justices were to be appointed by

---

[13] Tolman, *Municipal Reform Movements in the United States,* pp. 124-128.

[14] Howe, "Municipal History of New Orleans," pp. 186, 187.

[15] Devlin, *Municipal Reform in the United States,* pp. 49, 50; Conkling, *City Government in the United States,* p. 191.

[16] Tolman, *op. cit.,* pp. 81, 82.

[17] *Ibid.,* pp. 60, 61.

[18] MacLawrin, Donald D., "Municipal Conditions in Detroit," National Conference for Good City Government, *Proceedings for 1895,* p. 387.

the Mayor rather than elected by the people and had to be trained lawyers with at least five years' practice.[19]

Civil service was a popular cry with most of the reformers, but not until after 1890 did they make much headway in securing what could actually be called a merit system. After the Civil War all of the large cities were in the grip of the spoils system. It was the strongest weapon of the boss and a primary source of weakness to the city. Hand in hand with corruption went partisanship, whose "greatest toll was not through dishonesty but through inefficiency."[20] Frequent changes in the personnel of the staff, the appointment of men of mediocre ability and the creation of unnecessary offices to satisfy the job-seekers—all had a disastrous effect upon municipal administration. Although Charles Sumner had fought for civil service reform in the national government, scarcely a voice was raised in its favor in the cities for many years.[21] Only the most flagrant abuses attracted attention in the earlier days of reform. The tendency was to try to prevent improper removals rather than to secure proper appointments. As early as 1873 New York prohibited the removal of policemen and firemen except for a good cause.[22]

With the eighties civil service laws were passed by a few state legislatures. In most cases in which the laws applied to municipalities, they were mandatory for cities above a certain size; some cities had the right to select their own systems. After the organization of the National Civil Service Reform League in 1881, with 31 unit branches, information and propaganda on the merit system were widely disseminated through a monthly magazine called *Good Government*. By 1893 the League had a national membership of 10,000.[23]

New York led the way in 1883 with the first civil service law in any state; it was mandatory for cities of more than 50,000 and the Mayor was given power to prescribe the specific rules. The next generation continued the fight in New York for further extension of civil service and, by 1897, 35 cities were operating on the merit system.[24] Massachusetts followed New York with a general civil service law for state and cities in 1884. The bill intro-

---

[19] Eaton, *The Government of Municipalities*, p. 442.
[20] Griffith, *The Modern Development of City Government in the United Kingdom and in the United States*, pp. 153, 154.
[21] Munro, William Bennett, *The Government of American Cities* (New York, 1912), pp. 17, 18.
[22] *Ibid.*, p. 17.
[23] Tolman, *op. cit.*, pp. 121, 122; ante, pp. 31, 32.
[24] Woodruff, *"Progress of Municipal Reform,"* p. 313.

duced in the Maryland legislature that year failed to pass and was not approved until 1897.[25]

Among the first cities to incorporate civil service regulations in their charters was Philadelphia. The Bullitt Bill of 1885 gave the Mayor and the department heads power to make regulations for applications, examinations, and promotions, and to appoint a civil service board to administer such regulations.[26]

In the 1890's the spoils system was a favorite target for reform in cities. Within the span of a few years the number of states and cities with provisions for civil service reform doubled and re-doubled.[27] Many of the victories, however, were theoretical and short-lived. In practice politicians usually managed to circumvent the laws.[28] Chicago provided an elaborate merit system in 1895; in the next year Mayor Harrison opposed it strenuously and in the end appointed his own commissioner to the civil service board and filled 60% of the offices with his personal followers.[29] The merit system was included in the New Orleans charter of 1896, but was repealed in 1900 by the efforts of the politicians.[30] It is interesting to note that such large cities as St. Louis and Detroit entered the new century with no accomplishment whatever in the battle for civil service reform. In 1900 New York state could still claim the greatest advancement in civil service.[31]

Another field of battle in the struggle for better municipal administration was the fight against special privilege, monopoly, big business. While cities once had welcomed the corporations and granted unlimited favors, they now turned against them as objects of suspicion and persecution. By 1890 there was a noticeable change in public opinion; opposition to vested interests was growing stronger. People resented the firm grip of corporations upon the purse strings of their cities. Nor was the motive wholly economic. Was it not the bribes of public utilities that had planted the seeds of graft in the councils and courts? There was now no disposition on the part of the reformers to compromise with privilege.

---

[25] Shepard, Edward M., *The Competitive Test and the Civil Service of States and Cities* (New York, 1885), p. 14.

[26] Mercer, G. G., "Municipal Government of Philadelphia," National Conference for Good City Government, *Proceedings for 1894*, pp. 96, 97.

[27] Illinois, Indiana, Wisconsin, Milwaukee, Chicago, 1895; Louisiana, Seattle, Tacoma, New Orleans, 1896; Connecticut, Maryland, 1897.

[28] Schlesinger, *Rise of the City*, p. 394.

[29] Gregory, *Civil Service Reform in American Municipalities*, pp. 11, 12.

[30] *Ibid.*, p. 10.

[31] *Ibid.*, pp. 7-11.

As municipal ownership and operation increased, the chances for bribery in contract awards became more and more frequent. Speculative development was widespread. Franchises were distributed with little regard for the rights of the cities. When Van Wyck became Mayor of New York City in 1897, the American Ice Company secured exclusive control of the docks. Van Wyck, as was later revealed, had $620,000 in American Ice Company stock.[32] Boss Magee of Pittsburgh organized his Consolidated Traction Company with capital of $30,000,000 and a 950-year charter granted by the Council.[33]

Under-assessment of corporation property involved problems of taxation. In 1881 Virginia passed a law to reform the taxation of public service corporations by reserving to the state the right of assessment on the basis of the returns filed by the corporation. Levying of the tax remained in the hands of the city. By 1890 this transfer of the power of assessment to the state had become a common practice in the effort to solve the problem of competitive local under-assessment.[34]

The public utilities were responsible for frequent trouble between the state and the city over the regulation of rates and the right of granting franchises. From 1885 to 1887 gas and electric rates in Massachusetts were controlled by a state commission.[35] In Ohio a state board granted a 50-year street railway franchise for Cincinnati without allowing the city any right of interference.[36]

Chicago came to blows with the state legislature over the Allen Law of 1897, which raised the maximum period of the street railway franchise from 20 to 50 years. The bill was pushed through the legislature by Charles T. Yerkes, in spite of the protests of all the Chicago newspapers and the people as a whole. So much opposition arose that the obnoxious measure was repealed in 1899 and the former limit of 20 years restored.[37]

Anti-monopoly won its greatest victory of the period while Hazen S. Pingree was Mayor of Detroit from 1889 to 1897. "Pin-

[32] Werner, *Tammany Hall*, p. 466.

[33] Steffens, *The Shame of the Cities*, pp. 174-177. While from 1885 to 1897 horse vehicles paid taxes of $47,000 per year and bicycles paid $7,000, the Consolidated Traction Company paid only $9,600 per year. The speed of horse vehicles and bicycles was limited by law but the traction was unregulated. *Ibid.*, pp. 174-177.

[34] Griffith, *op. cit.*, pp. 84, 85.

[35] *Ibid.*, p. 98.

[36] Orth, Samuel Peter, *The Centralization of Administration in Ohio* (New York, 1903), p. 17.

[37] Ritchie, William, "The Street Railway Situation in Chicago," National Conference for Good City Government, *Proceedings for 1901*, pp. 165-168.

gree was but the first of many leaders of the new and critical democracy in local government."[38] His struggle against vested interests
was the beginning of a long battle in which others were inspired
to follow, "Golden Rule" Jones of Toledo, McKisson and Rose of
Cleveland, MacMurray of Denver, John Harland of Chicago,
Thomas L. Johnson of Cleveland. Pingree had his first chance to
attack public utilities during a strike of the traction employees.
He endorsed their conduct and the company came to terms. And
he persisted in his fight to lower the fares, improve the service,
limit the franchises, and in every way possible protect the public
against the encroachments of unfair privilege. He exposed grafting members of the council, wrung concessions from the gas company, and against ruthless opposition established a municipal light
plant. The corporations tried to enlist the legislature to block
Pingree's course, but without success. He was elected Governor
in 1896 and became a leader in the fight for direct primaries, corporation taxation, and regulation of public utility rates.[39]

Toledo was the scene of a struggle against big business when
"Golden Rule" Jones blocked the renewal of the street railway
franchise during his first administration.[40] The Council had granted
renewal for twenty-five years. Jones vetoed the measure, and
when they attempted to pass it over his veto, he rallied a crowd
and came to the Council meeting to protest. The Councilmen were
afraid to defy him in the face of the citizens. The attorney for the
street railway company said to Jones, as he left the meeting, "I
suppose, Mr. Mayor, that this is an example of government under
the Golden Rule." "No," replied Jones in a flash, "it is an example
of government under the rule of gold."[41]

Almost every city of size had some skirmish with monopoly,
as the occasion arose. G. W. Guthrie and W. B. Rogers led the
opposition in Pittsburgh in 1897 to the unfair contracts for the new
Public Safety Building.[42] In St. Louis J. W. Folk was stirring up
the secrets of the Central Traction Bill and exposing the scheme
of the United Railways for merger and monopoly.[43] The fear and
hatred of special privilege spread rapidly throughout the country.

In one sense of the word, the fight against big business was
a part of the whole effort to lower the cost of government. The

---

[38] Griffith, *op. cit.*, p. 157.
[39] *Ibid.*, pp. 156, 157; Schlesinger, *Rise of the City*, p. 393.
[40] *Ante*, p. 45.
[41] Whitlock, *op. cit.*, pp. 131, 132.
[42] Steffens, *op. cit.*, pp. 171, 172.
[43] *Ibid.*, pp. 50-56.

cities found themselves in 1875 with such appalling debts to carry that they could no longer neglect the question of municipal finance.[44] That was one matter that demanded immediate action. Furthermore, the running expenses of the cities were constantly increasing. The report of the New York Commissioners in 1876 revealed an increase in annual expenditures since 1850, as compared with the population, of 400%, 200%, as compared with the increase of taxable property.[45] Candidates for office began to find their strongest appeal to the people in a pledge of retrenchment and economy. Debt limitation, tax limitation, and scientific budgeting were all enlisted to meet the financial crisis.

One of the first and most extensive methods of financial control was the limitation of municipal debts by the state. By 1890, some 14 states had adopted measures to limit the borrowing power of their cities and towns.[46] The Illinois legislature in 1870 passed a debt limit of five percent of the assessed value of property, the loan to be paid up within 20 years.[47] In 1884 New York amended her tax and debt limit act of 1846, making it apply to cities of more than 100,000, with a debt limit of ten percent, a time limit of 20 years, and a tax limit of two percent.[48]

Tax limitation was likewise a popular economy measure. By 1890 ten states were regulating municipal taxation by constitutional provision.[49] There were difficulties in such state regulation, however, for growing cities needed more flexible provisions. Cases requiring popular sanction for debt or expenditure, as did Washington, D. C., found such regulation quite ineffective, for the people were usually the first to encourage new projects.[50]

To meet extreme emergencies a few cities, especially in the South, were forced to repudiate their debts. Selma and Mobile, Alabama, declared themselves bankrupt in 1878, as did Houston

---

[44] *Ante*, p. 10, 11.

[45] Bryce, *The American Commonwealth*, vol. 1, p. 643.

[46] New York, Maine, Illinois, Wisconsin, Iowa, West Virginia, Missouri, Pennsylvania, Georgia, Colorado, Oregon, California, Indiana, Arkansas. Fassett Committee, *Testimony Taken Before the Senate Committees on Cities, Pursuant to Resolutions Adopted January 20, 1890* (Albany, 1890), vol. 5, pp. 525-530; Griffith, *op. cit.*, pp. 69, 70.

[47] *Ibid.*, p. 26.

[48] *Ibid.*, p. 70.

[49] Illinois, Nebraska, West Virginia, North Carolina, Missouri, Arkansas, Texas, Alabama, Louisiana, New York. Fassett Committee, *op. cit.*, vol. 5, pp. 512-517.

[50] Porter, J. D., "The City of Washington: Its Origin and Administration," Johns Hopkins University, *Studies in Historical and Political Science*, vol. 3 (November and December, 1885), *passim*.

and Memphis.[51] Cairo, Illinois, stopped interest payments. Duluth paid 50 cents on the dollar. New Orleans and San Antonio had unusually fine records; both struggled under serious handicaps and paid off all debts.[52] In some cases municipal revenue was greatly increased by a system of license fees, as on saloons and public houses. In the ten years from 1880 to 1890 Chicago increased its receipts from licenses from $242,774 to $3,072,729.[53]

All of these attempts to lower the debt and increase the revenue met with varying degrees of success. Doubtless they were effective, on the whole, for the general cost of government declined between 1875 and 1900. While in 1880 the outstanding loans of American cities were $724,000,000 or $14.48 per capita, in 1890 they were only $781,000,000 or $12.40 per capita. In 1898 the municipal levy of Cleveland was $12.50, the lowest in its history. Expenses for such functions as sanitation, education, and charity were rising as the cities enlarged their programs, but the cost of administration itself had been successfully checked.[54]

But debt and tax limitation by the state was of temporary significance as compared with the introduction of scientific budgeting. Before 1870 the Council had had unlimited control of the budget. Now the states began to demand stricter regulation by law. Illinois in 1872 passed a measure for budget reform, Michigan in 1873, California in 1877, Nebraska in 1887, Montana in 1895.[55] The Illinois law, copied in principle by the others, stated that the object for appropriations must be specified, that additional expenditure must be approved by two-thirds of the council or by popular consent, and that no additional contracts could be made unless specified in the general appropriation.[56]

In 1870 New York City adopted a plan for a Board of Estimate and Apportionment, the majority of the members to be appointed by the Mayor. In origin the board was only a device of the Tweed Ring, but it proved to be a valuable method of finance control and was copied by Detroit in 1873. Some cities provided budget restriction by granting to the Comptroller power to check on the acts of the Council, as did Philadelphia in 1879 and Boston

---

[51]*Ante*, p. 16.
[52] Griffith, *op. cit.*, p. 66.
[53] Merriam, Charles Edward, *Report of an Investigation of the Municipal Revenues of Chicago* (Chicago, 1906), pp. 19-23.
[54] Griffith, *op cit*, p. 86.
[55] Clow, Frederick Redman, *A Comparative Study of the Administration of City Finances in the United States* (New York, 1901), p. 118.
[56] Griffith, *op. cit.*, p. 68.

in 1885.[57] In 1891 Buffalo authorized the Mayor to reduce or strike out items of which he did not approve.[58] Indianapolis in 1894 allowed the Comptroller and Mayor to make the budget with the Council acting merely as a board of review.[59] Thus in the larger cities there was a distinct tendency to deprive the Council of its former power in matters of expenditure and enhance the prerogatives of the Comptroller and Mayor. The development of scientific budget control provided one of the greatest safeguards to the municipal treasury and proved to be a most effective accomplishment in the effort to lower the cost of government.

---

[57] Ibid., p. 69.
[58] Larned, Josephus Nelson, A History of Buffalo, Delineating the Evolution of the City (New York, 1911), vol. 1, p. 195 ff.
[59] Clow, op. cit., p. 118 ff.

Chapter Six

Toward Better Living

IF the fight for better administration in city affairs—better officials, better elections, better control of finance—was the first field of battle for reformers, the second cause that claimed their loyalty was that of civic betterment. Theirs was the desire to make the city a decent, safe, and pleasant place in which to live. As the population grew and prosperity increased, the functions of the municipality multiplied rapidly, and with increased functions came increased responsibility and greater need of control. Altruism, community pride, and municipal rivalry became important factors in civic consciousness. Cities were boastful and proud when they could claim the best schools or the best parks in their state. In 1895 Boston boasted of the highest salaries for teachers in the world.[1] Functional development increased slowly after the Civil War, but during the last decade of the century it progressed with remarkable strides. People became alert to the need for parks, playgrounds, libraries, health service, tenement regulations, juvenile courts.

There seemed to be no limit to the types of civic betterment that were initiated by public and private agencies. In 1888 New York began the acquisition of the Bronx Park.[2] Boston opened public playgrounds in 1893 and launched plans for the extensive parkways advocated by Dr. Charles W. Eliot.[3] Baltimore established an Art Commission in 1890, a forerunner of city planning.[4] Juvenile courts were introduced in Massachusetts and New York in 1890.[5] Buffalo established a bacteriological laboratory.[6] Cleveland opened a department of forestry in 1897.[7] This period saw the beginning of large public benefactions, such as the Carnegie library appropriations. Between 1892 and 1902 private gifts to libraries totalled $46,136,485, of which Carnegie gave $31,075,000.[8]

These developments were luxuries, however, compared to the need

---

[1] Griffith, *The Modern Development of City Government in the United Kingdom and in the United States*, p. 103.

[2] Wright, Andrew, "The Development of Park Systems in America," American Academy of Political and Social Science, *Annals*, vol. 25 (March, 1905), p. 222.

[3] *Ibid.*, pp. 224, 225.

[4] Griffith, *op cit.*, p. 80.

[5] *Ibid.*, p. 83.

[6] Larned, *A History of Buffalo*, p. 172 ff.

[7] Orth, Samuel Peter, *A History of Cleveland, Ohio* (Cleveland, 1910), p. 176.

[8] Griffith, *op. cit.*, p. 83.

for the suppression of vice and the improvement of the moral tone of city life. One of the most ardent volunteers in the early days of the fight against vice was Anthony Comstock, founder of the Society for the Suppression of Vice, an organization launched in 1873.[9] He and his workers conducted extensive surveys of vice dens and so aroused public sentiment that the cost of the crusade, averaging $7,000 a year, was borne entirely by voluntary contributions. Between 1873 and 1881 they seized and destroyed 163 of the 165 plates then in use in connection with filthy literature, brought about the arrest of 650 persons and the closing of nine lotteries. More than 60 abortionists were arrested and all but a few convicted and sentenced. As a result of the efforts of the society the New York City government collected $63,931 in fines and $50,900 in forfeited bonds.[10] So effective was Comstock's work that he secured the passage of a law by Congress in 1873 to prevent the use of the mails for obscene literature and was appointed a special agent of the Post Office Department.[11]

There is a curiously interesting story in the work of Dr. Charles H. Parkhurst, whose intelligent and persistent efforts as a minister and president of the Society for the Prevention of Crime brought further results in New York's struggle with vice.[12] From his Madison Square Church pulpit in 1892 Dr. Parkhurst denounced the city administration for its protection of crime. The *Tammany Times* challenged the minister to prove his statements. So, disguised by work-a-day clothes, Dr. Parkhurst set out on a daring tour of New York's inferno, accompanied by Charles W. Gardner, a special detective. The two men visited Tom Summer's saloon, a five-cent lodging house, cabarets, Chinese opium dens, and such dens of prostitution as "Tight House" and the "Golden Rule Pleasure Club." Together they gathered incriminating evidence and demanded that the District Attorney and the courts follow up the evidence with strict enforcement of the law. At the Essex Market Court Parkhurst and Gardner were mobbed by a huge crowd after they had testified against disorderly houses and their keepers.[13] So startling were the facts uncovered by Parkhurst that the administration dared not defy public sentiment. Additional evidence began to be revealed by other reform agencies. Vice could never again be quite so safe and bold in New York. This crusade was one of the immediate causes for the appointment of the Lexow Committee, which made a complete investigation of law enforcement in New York City.

[9] *Ante*, p. 28.
[10] Comstock, and others, "The Suppression of Vice," pp. 484-489.
[11] Van Doren, "Anthony Comstock," p. 330.
[12] *Ante*, pp. 35, 36.
[13] Werner, *Tammany Hall*, pp. 348-355; Parkhurst, *My Forty Years in New York*, pp. 106-151.

Toledo's famous Mayor, "Golden Rule" Jones, was a leader in the effort to raise the moral tone of his community.[14] This big sandy Welshman was a wealthy business man. He always dressed in a broad-brimmed hat and flowing cravat. His motto—the Golden Rule—was constantly posted on the wall of his office. In endeavoring to humanize law enforcement, he improved the personnel of the police force, took away their clubs, visited the prisons and workhouses and talked with the men. Though opposed by business and ridiculed in the press, he was well loved by the lower classes, whose standard of life he tried hard to raise.[15]

Except for the efforts of a few outstanding individuals, most of the national fight against vice and the struggle for law enforcement was carried on by hundreds of organizations determined to make the cities decent places for family life. The work of such influential agencies as the Christian Endeavor Societies and the Citizens' Federation of Toledo in closing saloons and gambling houses exemplifies the methods of many reform groups.[16] The Citizens' Law and Order League of New Haven, Connecticut, secured the conviction of nearly 300 lawbreakers from the time of its organization in 1892 until 1895.[17]

Another field of effort in civic betterment during this period was the attempt to improve conditions of health and sanitation. Dr. Henry I. Bowditch of Boston made an extensive survey of the health conditions in the United States in 1877. He sent out a questionnaire to 179 leading medical doctors and recorded some startling results in his book, *Public Hygiene in America*. It was found that only twelve states reported expenditures of state money for boards of health, state and local; only twelve reported that money was granted for investigating the causes of disease. Of the 143 cities reported, 34.6% paid attention to purity of city water. Only thirteen states reported sewers to carry off water. Providence, Rhode Island, was the only city to have a perfect sewerage system. Indiana and Iowa in 1876 had no health legislation save for the protection of cattle. In Dallas, Texas, the members of the Board of Health resigned in 1876 because they could not command any attention from the city. Georgia in 1875 reported only five local boards of health in the entire state, while Baltimore was the only city in Maryland to have a Board of Health.[18]

Why did such conditions exist? They were due in part to the failure to understand the nature of disease. People were not disturbed about general health conditions until the 1880's, when the germ theory of disease

---

[14] *Ante*, p. 45.
[15] Whitlock, *Forty Years of It*, pp. 112-121.
[16] *Ante*, pp. 35-37.
[17] Tolman, *Municipal Reform Movements in the United States*, p. 101.
[18] Bowditch, Harry I., *Public Hygiene in America* (Boston, 1877), *passim.*

began to be well understood.[19] Once, however, citizens at large were convinced of the importance of city health, they wrung from their legislature the necessary power to combat the evils of infested sections. In New York City the Ladies' Health Protective Association was organized in November, 1884, for the express purpose of securing better sanitary laws and the enforcement of existing laws. With twelve committees, each in charge of some special phase of sanitation, the organization began an intensive campaign of investigation.[20]

A survey made by the Federal Government in 1893 exposed glaring facts which helped to open the eyes of the people about tenement conditions in New York, Philadelphia, Chicago, and Baltimore. The survey revealed that one-room tenements were occupied by an average of 13.16 persons in Baltimore, 12.10 in Philadelphia, 5.87 in Chicago, and 5.62 in New York.[21] In 1895 the citizens of New York City organized a Tenement House Committee and secured the recognition of the legislature for an official investigation of the housing conditions. Richard W. Gilder, editor of *Century,* was the chairman.[22] Definite results followed the investigation. In that same year the legislature provided $5,000,000 for park and recreation facilities and made the Board of Health responsible for sanitation and inspection.[23] In 1897 a medical inspector appeared in all the schools.[24] Meanwhile the Tenement House Committee called a mass meeting at Cooper Union on May 8, 1896, for the promotion of better housing —a movement which has seen rapid advancement in recent years.

Other cities were likewise paving the way toward sanitation reform. In 1893 there was organized the Philadelphia branch of the National Women's Health Protective Association for the purpose of investigating complaints about garbage collection and reporting to the police cases of neglect.

A law passed in the same year provided for wider recreation areas, better health facilities, inspection, and a Board of Health.[25]

The Women's Health Protective Association of Brooklyn was launched in 1890 to arouse women to their municipal obligations and to promote health and sanitation by seeing to it that the necessary laws were

[19] Schlesinger, *Rise of the City,* pp. 240-244.
[20] Tolman, *op. cit.,* p. 171.
[21] Weber, Gustavus A., "Improved Tenement Homes for American Cities," *Municipal Affairs,* vol. 1 (December, 1897), pp. 746, 747. In New York City in 1895 there were 50% of the population living in wards which were less than one-tenth of the area of the entire city. In 1894 it was reported that 1,487,392 people lived in 42,909 tenement houses. *Ibid.,* p. 746.
[22] Cadman, S. Parkes, "The Tenement House Reform in New York City," *Chautauquan,* vol. 25 (September, 1897), pp. 588, 589.
[23] Weber, G. A., *loc. cit.,* p. 748.
[24] Cadman, *loc. cit.,* p. 590; Griffith, *op. cit.,* p. 83.
[25] Tolman, *op. cit.,* pp. 173, 174; Weber, G. A., *loc. cit.,* p. 749.

passed and enforced. This organization of 450 members, with branch organizations in each ward, conducted a vigorous campaign and by 1893 reported that Brooklyn had cleaner streets and street-cars. Women had also contributed to the overthrow of the political ring in that city.[26]

In 1892 the Municipal Order League of Chicago was organized by women to promote sanitation.[27] By 1894 there was organized the Women's Health Protective Association to investigate school hygiene, tenement houses, and general sanitation.[28] A few years later, in 1897, the city passed laws condemning houses that were unfit to live in.[29]

In 1889 and 1891 Denver was given wide powers in the control of local health.[30] A few states made local Boards of Health mandatory, as did Massachusetts in 1895, New Jersey in 1880, Ohio in 1888.[31] In some of the Southern states the state Boards of Health had direct supervision over localities where the conditions were so serious that local governments could not cope with them. This was done in Louisiana, Georgia, and Alabama.[32]

All things considered, the signs of the times were pointed toward better municipal sanitary conditions. With all its handicaps, the reform movement of the nineteenth century offered the initial stimulus for a program of civic improvement that was to expand rapidly in the years ahead.

The period from 1875 to 1900 was one of vast improvement for the city schools. While the principle of free education was generally accepted by 1875, there was still much to be learned about its application and expansion. The number of public schools increased rapidly. In 1870 there were 160 public high schools in the country; in 1880 there were 800 and in 1890 there were 2,526. By 1900 the number had reached 6,005.[33] As the cities grew and the schools multiplied, local council committees proved entirely inadequate and incompetent for problems of school administration and school boards began to be freed from council control. Chicago in 1889 and Baltimore in 1898 provided that school boards be appointed by the Mayor. In 1897 Milwaukee placed school board appointments in the hands of a bi-partisan commission of four men, ap-

---

[26] Tolman, *op. cit.*, pp. 174-176.

[27] *Ibid.*, p. 171.

[28] Mumford, Mary E., "The Relation of Women to Municipal Reform," National Conference for Good City Government, *Proceedings for 1894*, p. 136.

[29] Weber, G. A., *loc. cit.*, p. 749.

[30] King, *The History of the Government of Denver*, p. 109.

[31] Orth, *The Centralization of Administration in Ohio*, p. 133.

[32] Griffith, *op. cit.*, p. 92.

[33] Dexter, Edwin Grant, *A History of Education in the United States* (New York, 1904), *passim*.

pointed by the Mayor, one from each ward.[34] In some instances Boards of Education were being endowed with financial power, not without strenuous opposition from the City Councils. Denver made such a provision in 1874 and in 1878 the Library Board of Cleveland, appointed by the Board of Education, was given separate taxing power.[35]

In addition to independent school boards, another advancement in educational supervision came when women were given the right to vote in school elections. Following the example of Kansas in 1861, Michigan and Minnesota granted woman suffrage in school elections in 1875 and by 1898 some 17 states and territories had made similar provisions.[36]

With better methods of school supervision, the educational system broadened its field and improved its curriculum. Public schools were extended to include kindergartens, normal schools, and night schools. Free kindergartens were especially popular, increasing from 459 in 1892 to 2,996 in 1901.[37] Twenty-one cities maintained normal schools in 1880, 44 cities in 1902. In the ten years from 1880 to 1890 the cities supporting night schools increased from 32 to 165. Until 1900 New York City was the only municipality to include free lectures in its educational system.[38] Keeping pace with the new educational theories, the public school curriculum was expanded to include such subjects as nature, drawing, music, manual training, technical courses, and hygiene.[39]

The idea of compulsory school attendance was gradually introduced and school laws made more stringent. By 1900 some 43 states had compulsory education laws.[40] Average daily attendance increased from 59.3% in 1870 to 68.6% in 1900.[41] School terms were lengthened from an average of 132.1 days in 1870 to 144.3 days in 1900.[42]

Attendant upon the improvement in the service rendered was a great increase in expenditures on education. In 1870 the expenses of public schools totalled $69,107,612, or $15.20 per pupil in average attendance. In the school year 1901 to 1902 public education cost $249,374,000, an average of $22.67 per pupil.[43] The educational development revealed by such facts as these was largely the result of the efforts of local reform organizations bent upon civic improvement from a cultural as well as political point of view.

---

[34] Griffith, *op. cit.*, p. 78.
[35] King, *op. cit.*, p. 76; Orth, *History of Cleveland, Ohio*, p. 253.
[36] Schlesinger, *Rise of the City*, p. 147.
[37] Dexter, *op. cit.*, p. 77.
[38] *Ibid.*, p. 77.
[39] Griffith, *op. cit.*, pp. 77, 78.
[40] *Ibid.*, p. 78.
[41] Dexter, *op. cit.*, p. 164.
[42] *Ibid.*, p. 164.
[43] *Ibid.*, p. 164.

To leave the battle for municipal reform here, having discussed the fight for better administration and the struggle for civic betterment, would be to leave it just where the average citizen of that period usually left it. Corruption in city offices, fraudulent elections, unfair privilege, vice, poor sanitation, all were very obvious, very unjust, and not to be countenanced any longer. That was as far as the average viewpoint went. And it was because of this circumstance that the early reform movement made no more headway than it did. There were very few persons who recognized that the evils of the day were not fundamental sources of the city's failure. The problem was being approached from the wrong angle; the product rather than the machinery was being attacked.

CHAPTER SEVEN

Improving the Framework

THE major difficulties arose out of the inadequacy of the framework of municipal government—out of confused charters that failed to fix responsibility, neglected to provide for growing needs, left too many elective officials, and permitted excessive state interference.[1] Of the large municipalities only Brooklyn (then an independent community) and Boston had by 1890 made any substantial progress in improving the form of city government.[2] During the last decade of the century, however, the old confusion began to clear and distinctly new tendencies became evident.

The need and the method of improvement were thrust forward by a perfectly natural series of events. The first step in this inevitable change was the decay and decline of the Council. As the city grew in complexity and its functions and duties multiplied, the old form of government, centering all activity in one body, broke beneath the load. It would have been unreasonable to have expected a superior group of men to administer all the details of a city, and the average Councilman was definitely far from superior. Under the increased burden, the Councils gave way to boards. The earlier boards were simply sub-committees of the Council, later they became separate boards appointed by the Council, and finally they became entirely independent. By such a process as this the Council was gradually deprived of its former significance.

Boston furnishes an excellent example of the decline of the Council. Until 1870 that city operated under a charter of 1854 restricting the authority of the Mayor and enhancing the rights of the Council. The Mayor's appointments were subject to the confirmation of the Aldermen. Although the Aldermen had full control of fire, police, health, markets, streets, and licenses, the Mayor had not even the right of veto. This was complete government by the

---

[1] Prior to 1890 there were still too many elective officials. The charter of Norfolk, Virginia, in 1882, left 20 officials to popular vote, in addition to the Mayor and Council. Among these were one weigher of hay, one gauger, one inspector of liquors. Griffith, *op. cit.*, p. 127. In Denver by 1885 there were 15 officials to be elected by popular vote. King, *The History of the Government of Denver*, p. 119 ff.

[2] Griffith, *The Modern Development of City Government in the United Kingdom and in the United States*, p. 124.

Council.[3] In 1870 the pendulum began to swing in the opposite direction. The legislature that year established a Board of Street Commissioners, to be elected by the people for a term of three years, and to have all the related power formerly held by the Aldermen. The following year the legislature created for Boston a Department for the Survey of Buildings, the chief to be appointed by the Mayor and Council. The Fire Department was taken from the Council in 1873 and given to three Commissioners, likewise appointed by the Mayor and Council. In 1875 the legislature provided for three Park Commissioners and three Water Commissioners, this time to be appointed by the Mayor and approved by the Council. A similar provision of 1878 called for three Commissioners to take charge of liquor traffic and the police. The climax to this whole series of measures was an act of 1885 which gave the entire executive power to the Mayor and deprived the Council of any part in administrative affairs. The Mayor was to appoint all boards, commissions, and committees.[4] This, then, was government by the Mayor and not by the Council.

Other cities evidenced the same trend. The idea was developing that municipal administration was far more a matter of business than a matter of government, and that a powerful but inefficient Council was simply not a good business proposition.[5] To meet this new idea the New Orleans charter of 1879 provided for an administrative system to include a Mayor and seven Administrators, elected on a general ticket. The Council was done away with completely. The seven Administrators were heads of the various city departments, and, with the Mayor, combined the powers of executive and Council.[6]

New York City offers a strange exception to the widespread tendency throughout the nation. While the New York charter prior to 1897 rendered the Council weak, there came a reaction in its favor and the new charter, by which Greater New York was created, increased the power of the Council.[7]

The general decline in the authority of the Council was accompanied by a corresponding decline in the type of men attracted to its service. There had never been a reasonable recompense; now, with authority taken away, there was not even the incentive of leadership or public duty. An inferior class of men in the Council

---

[3] Shepherd, H. N., *The Mayor and the City* (n. p., 1894), p. 87.
[4] *Ibid.*, pp. 87, 88.
[5] Goodnow, *City Government in the United States*, p. 139.
[6] *Ibid.*, p. 139.
[7] *Ibid.*, pp. 140-146.

chairs only increased the distrust of the people and encouraged
their inclination to make further limitations.[8]

The gradual shifting of authority led to the second inevitable
step toward an adequate framework for city government—the
demand for new charters to meet the new requirements. Here,
indeed, was a field for battle. Every reformer had his own idea
of what a model charter should be. One side advocated centralization of power in the Mayor, another side opposed it; one side
proposed a unicameral legislature, another branded it as dangerous.
As popular sentiment shifted, there were frequent charter changes.
It is not to be supposed that the features of the charters which are
today recognized as commendable were then generally agreed upon.
Such was not the case. Those charters were still experiments,
many of them successful and many unsuccessful. But while it is
true that the framework of municipal government had not arrived
at a distinctly new and better form by 1900, it is also true that in
the early charter experiments can be found some tendencies that
have survived and proved their worth.

The program adopted by the National Municipal League in
1898 included virtually all of the more advanced theories. The
League advocated among other things, the "Federal Plan" charter,
the short ballot, a wide measure of home rule, exemption from
debt limits of remunerative public works, a limited period of franchise, secret ballot, separate city and state elections, the merit
system, and the election of the Council at large with the principle
of continuity. While no one reform battle ever accomplished all
of these principles, they do indicate the trend that the new century
was to follow.[9] The Baltimore charter of 1898 contained principles
that were then the best in current thought. These principles may
be summed up in nine points: association of related branches of
municipal service into single departments, more appointive power
for the Mayor, representation of the minority party on all boards,
separation of municipal from state and national elections, employment of experts as heads of departments, awarding of franchises
to the highest bidder, a check on current expenditures and debt,
and non-political school control.[10]

---

[8] It is significant to note that in 1875 all the Aldermen of Boston owned
property with a total assessed value of $769,000, and 61 of the 74 Councilmen
owned property totalling $1,530,800. In 1892, however, 62 out of 87 Councilmen
owned no visible property, and in 1902 the total assessed valuation of the
property of both Aldermen and Councilmen was only $87,000. Griffith, *op. cit.*,
p. 111.

[9] *Ibid.*, pp. 161, 162.

[10] Hall, Clayton C., ed., *Baltimore: Its History and Its People* (New York,
1912), vol. 1, p. 304 ff.

The "Federal Plan" was one of the progressive features of many of the new charters. It was, in theory, the application of the national plan of separation of powers. In fact, it amounted to a recognition that the Mayor, as executive, should exercise more power. In 1878 Governor Hantranft of Pennsylvania advised a committee which was devising a plan of city government to uphold the American theory of the separation of powers. Philadelphia's Bullitt Charter of 1887 illustrated the attempt to copy closely the plan of our national government.[11] Cleveland adopted the "Federal Plan" in 1891 as a result of the pressure of business men upon the legislature. The Cleveland plan differed from that of Philadelphia in adapting the national principle to a simpler framework, copying the spirit rather than the letter.[12]

The bicameral Council was popular in many cases. All the cities in Pennsylvania had bicameral Councils after 1874. Indianapolis adopted the plan in 1877, Denver in 1885, Detroit in 1887.[13] In 1872 Illinois had provided for a general unicameral system for all cities. Chicago was divided on the question, one side favoring unicameralism and the other side bicameralism. An act calling for bicameral legislation was presented to the voters in 1875 and turned down. Friends of the measure claimed that the election was irregular but the court upheld it and the vote of the people stood in favor of unicameralism.[14]

St. Louis was the first city in the United States to frame its own charter. It did so in 1875 but within a few years a movement

---

[11] The similarity of plan may be illustrated by the following table:

United States	Philadelphia
President for four years.	Mayor for four years.
Two houses of Congress.	Two chambers.
Senate from each state.	Select Council from each ward.
House of Representatives according to population.	Common Council according to population.
Presidential message.	Mayor's message.
President's veto passed over by two-thirds vote.	Mayor's veto pased over by two-thirds vote.
President's appointments confirmed by Senate.	Mayor's appointments confirmed by Select Council.
President impeached by House of Representatives before Senate.	Mayor impeached by Common Council before Select Council.
Penalty—dismissal.	Penalty—dismissal.

Ashley, Percy, *Local and Central Government; a Comparative Study of England, France, Prussia and the United States* (New York and London, 1906), pp. 196, 197.

[12] Ritchie, *"Commercial Organizations and Municipal Reform,"* p. 119.
[13] Griffith, *op. cit.,* p. 114.
[14] Sparling, Samuel Edwin, *Municipal History and Present Organization of the City of Chicago* (Madison, Wis., 1898), pp. 60-65.

began for elaborate amendments. Thirty-six proposals for amendments were submitted to the citizenry in 1879; all failed to obtain the necessary two-thirds vote. Thirteen proposals were rejected in 1881, and seven in 1885. In October, 1885, after considerable modification, six amendments were finally accepted. The year 1888 saw two more defeated. In 1891 one proposal was ratified, providing for a sinking fund. The whole series of rejections was, in fact, a victory for the people. The proposed amendments had been hastily drawn up in an attempt to give more power to a few officials. A commission was appointed in 1895 to study the charter and report on its needs. But the commission was also a party strategy and simply offered amendments that would have given to the Council more power to make special assessments for public improvements. The newspapers and civic societies vigorously opposed these proposals and when they were submitted to popular vote in 1898, they were defeated by a great majority. Thus did St. Louis score another victory for municipal reform.[15]

The citizens of Pittsburgh were less successful in their attempts at charter reform. The old charter, granted in 1816, concentrated all power, executive, administrative, and legislative, in the Councils, with no separate departments. In 1887 Pittsburgh obtained a new charter, centering all executive and administrative power in the Mayor, the heads of departments to be elected by the Council. While in most cities such a charter would probably have been appropriate, in Pittsburgh, where the Magee-Flinn ring was so strong, the increased power of the Mayor was simply another source of evil to the reformers. With the defeat of G. W. Guthrie, reform candidate for Mayor in 1896, Matthew Quay, the state boss, sided with the reformers and promised to see that the legislature passed a new charter for Pittsburgh. The Municipal League and the Chamber of Commerce sent special committees to Harrisburg to urge the passage of the bill. It survived a first and second reading; then a change came. Quay saw that if he hoped to go to the United States Senate he must be careful with his enemies. Magee and Flinn were strong here, as well as at home. In the end Quay went to the Senate and the Pittsburgh charter failed.[16]

One further instance of charter changes is worthy of note. The tragic flood which killed one-sixth of the population of Galveston in 1900 was an emergency that demanded immediate

---

[15] Altman, Orven Roland, *Problems of Government in the St. Louis Metropolitan Area* (unpublished M. A. dissertation, University of Illinois, 1927), pp. 21, 22.

[16] Steffens, *The Shame of the Cities*, pp. 153, 154, 180-183.

changes in the administrative system. To meet the situation the people locked arms and commissioned five men to take full charge of the city government. In 1901 the commission form of government was incorporated in the Galveston charter, the first of its kind in the United States.[17]

The distinguishing feature of most of the new charters was the increase in the power of the Mayor, resulting in the rise of a better and stronger type of executive. In spite of the opposition of Councils and boards, whose authority was threatened, and in spite of the distrust of those who feared an "autocrat," greater duties were continually being placed upon the Mayor in the effort to create a responsible form of government. The first gain in most cases was the control over the budget.[18] New York City granted budget control to its Mayor as early as 1870; Detroit followed in 1873.[19] Police control was granted to Milwaukee's Mayor in 1874; Chicago made a similar provision the next year.[20] The veto power was given to the Mayor of Pittsburgh in 1874.[21] Under the St. Louis charter of 1875 the Mayor could veto entire bills or items of bills, a two-thirds vote of the Council being required to override his veto.[22]

More significant than any of these, however, was the increase in appointive power. Prior to 1882 the extension of appointive power was very gradual, the Mayor's decision, in most cases, being subject to the approval of the Council. In 1882 Brooklyn did away with the confirmation of the Mayor's appointments by the Council and that community's Mayor became the first really independent Mayor in the United States.[23] Seth Low was the first Mayor under the new plan; his administration has been designated as one of the best examples of the triumph of a good executive.[24] Other cities imitated the "Brooklyn Plan": New York in 1884, Buffalo in 1891, Louisville in 1893, New Haven in 1897, St. Paul, Duluth, and San Francisco in 1900.[25] In 1885 Boston granted the Mayor the additional right of removal, as did Denver in the same year and New York in 1896.[26] A bill giving the Mayor power to remove heads of

[17] Faulkner, *Quest for Social Justice*, p. 100.
[18] *Ante*, pp. 53, 54.
[19] Griffith, *op. cit.*, p. 118.
[20] Larson, "*A Financial and Administrative History of Milwaukee*," p. 106.
[21] Griffith, *op. cit.*, p. 109.
[22] Altman, *op. cit.*, p. 19.
[23] Griffith, *op. cit.*, p. 119.
[24] Orth, *The Boss and the Machine*, p. 55; *ante*, pp. 39, 40.
[25] Griffith, *op. cit.*, p. 119.
[26] *Ibid.*, p. 119.

departments was passed by the New York legislature but was vetoed by Governor Flower in 1894.[27]

The privileges of the chief executive were extended in many other ways. In 1885 Denver made the Mayor an ex officio member of all Council committees, and Boston required his approval for contracts of more than $2,000.[28] Cleveland in 1891 gave the Mayor power to appoint the six department heads and with them to revise ordinances of the Council.[29]

And so although the Mayor had not become absolutely dominant by 1900 either in theory or in practice, the trend toward a stronger executive had at least proved the gain of the new method. In 1880 only one of the 23 principal cities, New York, was dominated by a Mayor; 17 were controlled by Councils, three by independent boards, and two, New Orleans and Washington, D. C., by a form approaching commission government. By 1890 six, four of them the largest cities, had centered authority in the Mayor, eleven were still dominated by Councils, five by boards, and one, Washington, by a commission. During the last decade there was a marked increase in the Mayor's power, the number of cities in which he dominated being increased to twelve by 1900.[30]

One of the finest results of the extension of the Mayor's power was the fact that an entirely different and a far better type of man was attracted to the office. No longer was the Mayor a mere figurehead of the machine. He must be willing to shoulder responsibility and to answer for his every move. The Mayor appeared as a protector of the people's rights. Re-elections were frequent. Among the Mayors serving ten years or more were Doyle of Providence (1864 to 1869, 1871 to 1881, and 1887 to 1889); Latrobe of Baltimore (1875 to 1885 and 1887 to 1889); Harrison of Chicago (1879 to 1887, and 1893); and Haynes of Newark (1884 to 1894).[31]

Carter Harrison of Chicago was an interesting and powerful executive. He served from 1879 to 1887 and again in 1893. He bridged the gap from the fire to the fair.[32] He would not tolerate a boss nor permit organized political corruption. He was opposed by both the press and the reformers but the people voted for him because he did his work and protected their interests. After his

---

[27] Conkling, *City Government in the United States*, p. 33.
[28] Griffith, *op. cit.*, p. 119.
[29] *Ibid.*, p. 119.
[30] *Ibid.*, pp. 119, 120.
[31] *Ibid.*, p. 115.
[32] Merriam, *Chicago: A More Intimate View of Urban Politics*, p. 19.

assassination the Council became corrupt and remained so until Cole and the Municipal League won control.[33] The Harrison dynasty extended over ten terms, for Carter Harrison, Jr. served as Mayor for 1897 to 1903, and again from 1911 to 1915.[34]

The predominant leadership of Hazen S. Pingree of Detroit in the fight against monopoly has already been discussed.[35] Pingree served four terms, 1889 to 1897, and his masterful personality made him one of the strongest Mayors of his time. He received wide publicity in 1894 and 1895 for his "Potato Patch Plan" to aid the unemployed. He used the vacant city lots for raising potatoes and in the first year made a profit of $10,400, helping 943 families. The second year the project brought $22,100 profit and aided 1546 families.[36]

The closing years of the nineteenth century were climaxed by the administrations of such fine and efficient men as Strong of New York, Jones of Toledo, and Quincy of Boston.

As one reviews the accomplishments of the last quarter of the nineteenth century, one can see that a great reform was needed —that of home rule. A sad feature of the reform era was the fact that little was achieved in this connection. The basic principle of home rule was that the city should secure from the state the privilege of framing its own charter and conducting its affairs according to its own plans. Such a right would mean that the people themselves would make local regulations and local appointments, and that the state would not burden the city with excessive legislation.[37]

Efforts to secure home rule were largely local in origin and thus the battle recurred from time to time. On this question the machine and the reformers sometimes had much in common. When popular opinion opposed state interference strongly, almost any party with the necessities of a political force could offer to break the yoke that bound the city to the legislators and could usually count on winning the election. Thus home rule became a frequent rallying cry.[38]

Prior to 1875 a number of states had considerably limited the

[33] *Ibid.*, pp. 20, 21; *ante,* p. 40.

[34] Merriam, *Chicago: A More Intimate View of Urban Politics*, p. 21.

[35] *Ante,* pp. 50, 51.

[36] Haynes, Fred E., *Social Politics in the United States* (New York, 1924), p. 173.

[37] MacVeagh, "A Programme of Municipal Reform," *American Journal of Sociology,* vol. 1 (March, 1896), p. 554.

[38] Griffith, *op. cit.*, p. 148.

jurisdiction of the legislatures in city affairs.[39] Between 1875 and 1889 a distinct movement against partisan and special legislation and in favor of more home rule was noticeable, due perhaps to a calmer tone of national politics and a revulsion from the extreme measures of the previous decade.[40] The reformers were agitating for greater freedom and state legislatures began to realize that city supervision took too much time and interfered with other more pertinent problems demanding their attention.[41]

The first city to get home rule in the United States was St. Louis. In the years immediately prior to 1875, that city had not enjoyed the prosperity and civic improvement that it should have had. Taxes were high and the government was so deeply in debt that it had difficulty in paying the interest charges. In addition to a standing debt of $17,000,000, the city was compelled to issue anticipation bonds to meet current expenses. All those citizens really interested in their community's welfare had agreed by 1875 that some drastic changes ought to be made at once.

The doctors who diagnosed the ills of St. Louis were almost unanimous in the belief that the prime source of the civic malady was the domination and despotism of the state legislature. City officials were mere puppets in the hands of the state. Desiring more freedom, the delegates of St. Louis to the State Constitutional Convention in 1875 demanded home rule for their community. The suggestion was strongly opposed at first by the recalcitrant rural delegates, but by compromise it was ultimately achieved. The convention decided to grant the right to frame their own charters to all cities having a population of over 100,000. This privilege, however, did not affect any city at that time, as special provision was made for St. Louis, then the only city of the prescribed population.[42] Largely through the pressure from the German element, the freedom granted the city likewise separated it from the control of the county officials. On October 30, 1875, the Constitutional Convention granted St. Louis a divorce from both state and

---

[39] Committee of the National Municipal League, *A Municipal Program* (New York, 1899), p. 23. The states passing constitutional provisions limiting certain special legislation were Ohio and Virginia, 1851; Iowa and Kansas, 1860; Florida, 1865; Nebraska, 1867; Arkansas, 1868; Illinois, 1870; West Virginia, 1872; Texas and Pennsylvania, 1873. *Ibid.*, p. 24.

[40] *Ibid.*, p. 23.

[41] Utley, Henry Munson and Cutcheon, Byron M., *Michigan as a Province, Territory and State, The Twenty-Sixth Member of the Union* (New York, 1906), vol. 4, p. 218.

[42] Altman, *op. cit.*, pp. 14-16; Snow, Marshall S., "The City Government of St. Louis," Johns Hopkins University, *Studies in Political and Social Science*, vol. 5 (April, 1887), pp. 15-18.

county. The measure was ratified in 1876 by a majority of the city electorate.[43]

Excellent progress was made by St. Louis until Boss Butler came into power and cast an unfortunate reflection upon the name of home rule. It was not until 1914 that the city was able to develop a first-class governmental system.

Before 1900 four states had granted home rule to cities of certain sizes.[44] In addition to Missouri, California granted this privilege in 1879 to cities with populations of 3,500 or more; Washington to cities of 20,000 in 1889; Minnesota in 1896 to all cities.[45] Naturally, most cities did not hesitate to take advantage of the new freedom. Among the first communities in these states to secure their freedom were Tacoma and Seattle in 1890 and St. Paul in 1897.[46]

It is significant to note that home rule made its greatest gains in the West. The Old South did not seem to demand relief from state centralization, partly because the cities relied upon the states to insure their freedom from Negro interference. In 1881 and 1888 the states of Tennessee and South Carolina passed laws to tighten up the relations between states and cities. There was no strong opposition.[47]

The bitterest contest for home rule was waged in the East, but absolute freedom was not accomplished. In New York Governor Tilden in his annual message to the legislature in 1875 described the conditions in New York City and pointed out how the state had interfered in the affairs of the city for partisan purposes.[48] In the Governor's message of May 11, 1875, on municipal reform he urged home rule and separate elections.[49] In a Mayoralty address delivered on January 3, 1881, William Grace of New York City urged home rule for the city, and in his message of January 2, 1882, he demanded that local self-government be granted, pointing out that other needed reforms could not be accomplished without it. After four years' experience Mr. Grace gave his

[43] Altman, *op. cit.*, p. 17.
[44] Faulkner, *Quest for Social Justice*, p. 103.
[45] DeWitt, Benjamin Park, *The Progressive Movement: A Non-Partisan, Comprehensive Discussion of Current Tendencies in American Politics* (New York, 1925), p. 287.
[46] Griffith, *op. cit.*, p. 148.
[47] *Ibid.*, p. 99.
[48] Committee on Press and Literature of the Citizens' Union of New York City, *Home Rule in Cities* (n. p., n. d.), p. 4.
[49] *Ibid.*, p. 5.

opinions on local government and among the principal needs he still advocated home rule as the greatest need for his city.[50]

Before the Constitutional Convention of New York met in 1894, the Citizens' Union, an organization promoting the cause of home rule in New York City, drafted a bold circular on the subject and broadcast it widely. The circular bore these words in large letters, "Serve the People and not the Political Machine." Readers were urged to enroll in the Union and fight for the home rule cause.[51] In due time the Committee of Seventy adopted home rule measures in its Anti-Tammany platform and endorsed the candidates who adhered to such a program, especially W. L. Strong.[52]

These efforts were somewhat effective, for the president of the Constitutional Convention, Joseph H. Choate, reported for home rule. It was not passed however. The nearest approach was the incorporation in the state Constitution of a law providing that any special legislation must be approved by the Mayor but if the Mayor vetoed the measure it could be passed over his veto by the legislature.[53]

In the 1890's much attention was given to municipal reform in Ohio, for that state granted enlarged powers to its cities, and partial home rule to Cleveland, Cincinnati, Springfield, and Youngstown.[54] But Toledo was not granted the desired privileges enjoyed by its sister cities. The fight for home rule in Toledo was waged by Mayor Samuel Jones and what was gained by that city was due to his vigorous efforts. The opportunity came when the state had taken the appointment of the police away from the Mayor and placed it in the hands of a state commission. A similar event had occurred in Cincinnati and the right of the state to appoint a police commission had been sustained by the state Supreme Court. Now, when Mayor Jones was deprived of his power in this capacity, he contended it was a violation of the city's rights and he refused to surrender his power to the state commission. He consulted his friend, Brand Whitlock, who later became Mayor of Toledo, and was advised to fight the case out in the courts. Whitlock and Clarence Brown took charge of the case and won the decision handed down by the state Supreme Court. Thus the doc-

---

[50] *Ibid.*, pp. 5-7.
[51] *Ibid.*, pp. 12-21.
[52] *Ibid.*, pp. 21, 22.
[53] *Ibid.*, p. 15; Griffith, *op. cit.*, p. 148. The reform candidate for Mayor, W. L. Strong, won the Mayoralty contest in 1894 and was a constant fighter for more home rule.
[54] "The Key to Municipal Reform," *Century*, vol. 42 (October, 1891), p. 953.

trine in previous cases was overthrown and the whole fabric of municipal legislation in Ohio was affected.[55] This was the beginning of a great battle to be waged for home rule in the next century in Ohio.

Other cities put in their bid for independence. Governor Russell of Massachusetts in 1893 continually kept up agitation against state usurpation of municipal functions, but without results.[56] Louisiana in 1879 and 1886 conferred partial home rule upon its leading cities. At best there was nothing more than a general tendency toward decentralization from 1875 to 1900. Where the cities had bowed to the state in 1875, they were gaining more freedom by 1900, either by partial home rule or by using state boards only in an advisory capacity. It is quite obvious that the cities should have been left alone to work out their own salvation. The tendency toward more freedom forecast the new era of municipal reform to be continued in the twentieth century.

These, then, were the outstanding accomplishments along the fighting line for municipal reform from 1875 to 1900.

---

[55] Whitlock, *Forty Years of It,* pp. 135-137.
[56] Hennessy, Michael E., *Twenty-Five Years of Massachusetts Politics from Russell to McCall 1890-1915* (Boston, 1917), p. 37.

Chapter Eight

A Survey and Critical Analysis

CHARLES A. DANA of the *New York Sun* used to ridicule feeble reform efforts, dubbing them "the infantile blubber of the goo-goos," but as one pieces together the scattered details of the battle for municipal reform from 1875 to 1900, one is prompted to conclude that the blubber, futile as it often seemed, was doubtless a normal and inevitable precursor of what finally became, in the new century, a studied pronouncement of decent standards in municipal government. Amateur experiments are common forerunners of scientific advances. The amateur reformers of the last quarter of the nineteenth century, though handicapped by their own shortsightedness, deserve credit for the first general housecleaning in city affairs. Their grim struggle for elementary decency in city government opened the door for the later and more mature approach to municipal administration.

These amateurs are not to be blamed for their inefficency, but rather excused. The problem was new; few people understood its depth. What the cities needed was no one specific cure but a whole readjustment of civic and political standards to the new conditions of life. It was not purely a governmental question, but a complexity of social, economic, and political entanglement. With the industrialization that followed the Civil War there had come a rapid growth in city population, an extravagant program of public improvements, and a spirit of materialism in a citizenry preoccupied with the exploitation of a continent. The old framework of city government was not strong enough to carry the new burden and it became increasingly helpless as excessive state interference grew more and more intolerable. Into the gap left by an indifferent electorate and a weak charter that failed to fix responsibility stepped the political boss and his machine, ready to fill their pockets as donors of appointments and allies of big business.

In the face of such conditions as these began the agitation for reform. A machine, once in power, was difficult to dislodge. Politicians could devise tricks for winning votes faster than the public conscience could counteract them. Citizens were usually aroused to fight because of the obvious need for better administration.

First, they struggled to break the power of machine politics by exposing corrupt officials and instituting election and civil service reforms. Then they sought to lower the cost of administration by debt limitation and budgeting. Later, they endeavored to achieve civic betterment through law enforcement, sanitary improvements, and educational advancement.

As functions multiplied and the inadequacy of the old Council form of government came into glaring evidence, the new charters tended to increase the power and responsibilty of the Mayor. The rise of a better type of executive was a great accomplishment of the period. The fight against state interference, however, was only partially achieved. In the West came considerable progress in the latter field, but in 1900 only four states had granted complete home rule to their cities.

The strength of boss rule and the grip of organized wealth made early reform efforts look hopelessly weak and ineffectual. Reform groups, quick to strike at isolated evils but slow to recognize the fundamental causes of city failure, relied upon fitful and spasmodic rebellion rather than upon steady pressure. It was characteristic of early local reformers to spend much of their energy in stirring up excitement, calling great mass meetings, bemoaning political abuses, hailing a new era of good government, and then wondering which way to turn. When their first enthusiasm subsided, there was nothing left. They failed to see that real reforms move slowly, by constant, steady effort. There was, moreover, a regrettable lack of co-ordination and co-operation in the whole movement. The same problem, the same resistance, the same mistakes occurred again and again, but no one seemed to profit by the lessons learned.

Not until 1890 did the reform movement become a positive force in the adjustment of the municipal problem. Then, out of the mass of scattered experiences, there emerged material for analysis; local government became a laboratory of political and social experimentation. The importance of the founding of the National Municipal League in 1894 lies in the fact that it signified the rising strength of public opinion and the recognition of a new reform method. It is significant that in the same year the University of Pennsylvania created the first American lectureship in municipal government.[1] Public school "civics" began to shift its emphasis from national to local issues.

The studied analysis of the evils of city government was a new approach. It was the most enduring achievement of the reform era. The first feverish housecleaning had left the cities by no means immaculate, but at least they had been made clean enough for men to begin to think of making them cleaner and better. Thus, while the battle for municipal reform from 1875 to 1900 could claim few decisive victories, it gave rise to a moral awakening of the masses, a new civic consciousness, and a science of municipal government. The "blubber of the goo-goos" evolved into the clearer voice of a new century.

---

[1] The National Municipal League in 1900 made a survey of the study of municipal government in colleges and reported that, out of 222 schools scattered over the country, 42, or 19%, gave courses in municipal government, that 174, or 78%, gave courses in political science, and that 130, or 59%, gave courses in American government. Drown, Thomas M., "Report of the Committee on Instruction in Municipal Government in American Colleges," Rochester Conference for Good City Government, *Proceedings for 1901*, pp. 218-222.

APPENDIX

Bibliography

PRIMARY MATERIAL

BOOKS

Bowditch, Henry Ingersoll, *Public Hygiene in America.* Boston, 1877.
Based upon an extensive survey of health conditions in the United States.

Committee of the National Municipal League, *A Municipal Program.* New York, 1900.
Outlines the scheme of government proposed by the League.

Devlin, Thomas C., *Municipal Reform in the United States.* New York, 1896.
Urges reform in election system and civil service; approach is very good.

Ivins, W. M., *Machine Politics and Money in Elections in New York City.* New York, 1887.
A keen observer states the situation in New York City.

Matthews, Nathan, *The City Government of Boston.* Boston, 1895.
A Mayor of Boston from 1891 to 1895 presents his personal views as well as an explanation of his city's government.

Parkhurst, Dr. Charles H., *My Forty Years in New York.* New York, 1923.
One chapter gives a vivid account of the attack on Tammany from 1892 to 1894.

Steffens, Lincoln, *The Shame of the Cities.* New York, 1904.
A contribution to the literature of awakening and an invaluable account of the late period. Steffens has been called "The Prince of the Muckrakers."

Tolman, William Howe, *Municipal Reform Movements in the United States.* New York, 1895.
Contains a chapter by Rev. Parkhurst, who fought the corrupt element. The chapters by Tolman, secretary of the City Vigilance League, are lacking in facts. Contains valuable accounts of reform organizations and their objectives.

Vickers, George, *The Fall of Bossism. A History of the Committee of One Hundred and the Reform Movement in Philadelphia and Pennsylvania.* Philadelphia, 1883.
A very detailed and valuable book about the struggle for good government in Philadelphia.

77

Whitlock, Brand, *Forty Years of It*. New York, 1914.
An interesting and sympathetic account of Altgeld and his struggle with the Chicago Gas Ring. The account of "Golden Rule" Jones is charming and valuable.

ARTICLES

Baer, John Willis, "The Work of Christian Endeavor Societies in Behalf of Better Citizenship," National Conference for Good City Government, *Proceedings for 1895,* pp. 517-523.

Bemis, Edward W., "Local Government in Michigan and the Northwest," *Journal of Social Science,* vol. 17 (May, 1883), pp. 49-69.

Bowles, Samuel, "Relation of State to Municipal Government and the Reform of the Latter," *Journal of Social Science,* vol. 9 (January, 1878), pp. 140-146.
A very good analysis of the condition of city government; advocates a strong centralized system of state control.

Bradford, Gamaliel, "The Proposed Charter for the City of Boston," *North American Review,* vol. 123 (July, 1876), pp. 1-25.
A scorching review of the charter and reasons why it should be rejected.

Cadman, S. Parkes, "The Tenement House Reform in New York City," *Chautauquan,* vol. 25 (September, 1897), pp. 587-592.
Notes the difficulties of the problem, but deals principally with work that had been done.

Comstock, Anthony, and others, "The Suppression of Vice," *North American Review,* vol. 135 (November, 1882), pp. 484-501.
A fine review of the history of the society and its work in New York City.

Crandon, Frank D., "Misgovernment of Great Cities," *Popular Science Monthly,* vol. 30 (January, 1887), pp. 296-310, and (February, 1887), pp. 520-529.
A sound study of the ills of city government and their remedies.

Drown, Thomas M., "Report of the Committee on Instruction in Municipal Government In American Colleges," Rochester Conference for Good City Government, *Proceedings for 1901,* pp. 218-225.

Eaton, Dorman B., "Municipal Government," *Journal of Social Science,* vol. 5 (1873), pp. 1-35.
A lecture delivered before the Social Science Assembly in Boston, 1873. The author gives many general suggestions as to what he thinks city government should be.

Godkin, E. L., "A Key to Municipal Reform," *North American Review,* vol. 151 (October, 1890), pp. 422-431.

Godkin, E. L., "Criminal Politics," *North American Review*, vol. 150 (June, 1890), pp. 706-723.
A vigorous attack on the use made of the foreign element by politicians in New York.

Godkin, E. L., "The Last Attempt at Municipal Reform," *Nation*, vol. 28 (May 15, 1879), pp. 331-332.
Contends that the foreign element was a factor in support of the bosses; criticises the *New York Times* for advocating a great administration to be carried out by the reform candidate, Cooper. Out-and-out reform urged.

Gray, J. H., "Problems of Municipal Government," *Journal of Social Science*, vol. 34 (1896), pp. 174-181.
The problems are economic questions; nothing new is offered.

Guthrie, George W., "Municipal Conditions of Pittsburgh," National Conference for Good City Government, *Proceedings for 1896*, pp. 146-161.
An account of the conditions as related by an eye witness.

Harris, Daniel L., "Municipal Economy," *Journal of Social Science*, vol. 9 (January, 1878), pp. 147-163.
Contains a good analysis of the cost of city government in Springfield, Massachusetts.

Howard, C. M., "The Recent Revolt in Baltimore: Its Results and Lessons," National Conference for Good City Government, *Proceedings for 1896*, pp. 75-87.

Ivins, William M., "Municipal Finance," *Harpers*, vol. 69 (October, 1884), pp. 779-787.

Ivins, William M., "Municipal Government," *Political Science Quarterly*, vol. 2 (June, 1887), pp. 289-312.
Claims that changes in municipal organization have been incident to the extension of the general functions of government and gives an analysis of the system of government in New York City.

Kasson, John A., "Municipal Reform," *North American Review*, vol. 137 (September, 1883), pp. 218-230.
Presents some valuable statistics from the census; deplores the idea of extending the suffrage.

Lawson, Albert G., "A Christian Citizenship League," National Conference for Good City Government, *Proceedings for 1896*, pp. 275-282.
Deals with the organization of a new force to combat the evils in city government.

Lindsay, S. M., "Municipal Enterprises for Profit," *Journal of Social Science*, vol. 34 (1896), pp. 154-161.
A general discussion of public ownership.

Malone, James H., "Municipal Conditions of Memphis, Tennessee," National Conference for Good City Government. *Proceedings for 1896*, pp. 110-116.
Shows how state interference in Memphis was justified.

Mayors of Boston, et al., "How to Improve Municipal Government," *North American Review*, vol. 153 (November, 1891), pp. 580-595.
A good discussion on the Council and how to improve it.

Mercer, George Gluyas, "Municipal Government of Philadelphia," National Conference for Good City Government, *Proceedings for 1894*, pp. 94-102.

Mowry, Duane, "Reform and Reformers," *The American Magazine of Civics*, vol. 7 (November, 1895), pp. 462-465.
Mowry, a lawyer, declares that a professional reformer is a dangerous man.

Mumford, Mary E., "The Relation of Women To Municipal Reform," National Conference for Good City Government, *Proceedings for 1894*, pp. 135-143.
A valuable article showing how women aided the cause of good government.

"Municipal and Federal Reform," *Nation*, vol. 31 (December 30, 1880), pp. 454-456.
A vigorous article comparing the position of the New York Mayor with the President of the United States; accuses both of intriguing with bosses, especially Mayor Cooper, elected in 1878.

MacLawrin, Donald D., "Municipal Conditions in Detroit," National Conference for Good City Government, *Proceedings for 1895*, pp. 382-390.
One of the few accounts of the struggle between citizens and the machine for judicial reform.

MacVeagh, Franklin, "A Programme of Municipal Reform," *The American Journal of Sociology*, vol. 1 (March, 1896), pp. 551-563.
The founder of the Chicago Civic Federation gives an excellent examination of the faults in the existing system and suggestions for its improvement.

McKelway, St. Clair, "Modern Municipal Reform," *Journal of Social Science*, vol. 34 (1896), pp. 126-139.
The author seems to think reform has come to stay; he urges further reform in home rule.

"Organized Municipal Reform," *Century*, vol. 41 (March, 1891), pp. 789-790.
Advocates municipal elections at times other than state elections; praises the reform Mayors elected in Boston and Providence.

Parton, James, "Municipal Government," *Chautauquan,* vol. 8 (January, 1888), pp. 203-204.
A plea to make public office more desirable for able men.

Pingree, Hazen S., "The Problem of Municipal Reform. Contract by Referendum," *Arena,* vol. 17 (April, 1897), pp. 707-710.
Advocates a plan to improve city government, a scheme for which he fought while Mayor.

Pomeroy, Eltweed, "The Doorway of Reform," *Arena,* vol. 17 (April, 1897), pp. 713-721.
Few articles are more bitter than this diatribe against centralization in city government. The statistics on non-voting are most valuable.

Quinby, Isaac N., "Municipal Conditions of Jersey City," National Conference for Good City Government, *Proceedings for 1895,* pp. 353-357.
A good discussion of how Jersey City made progress in spite of legislative interference.

Ritchie, Ryerson, "Commercial Organizations and Municipal Reform," National Conference for Good City Government, *Proceedings for 1897,* pp. 118-127.
Explains cooperation between the City Council and the Chamber of Commerce, as in Cleveland.

Ritchie, William, "The Street Railway Situation in Chicago," National Conference for Good City Government, *Proceedings for 1901,* pp. 164-178.
An excellent account of the fight against franchises, especially against the Allen Bill of 1897.

Robbins, Mary Caroline, "Village Improvement Societies," *Atlantic Monthly,* vol. 79 (February, 1897), pp. 212-222.
An intelligent review of the origin and work of the societies in question.

Shaw, Albert, "Notes on City Government in St. Louis," *Century,* vol. 30 (June, 1896), pp. 253-264.

Teall, Oliver Sumner, "Municipal Reform," *Cosmopolitan,* vol. 10 (March, 1891), pp. 564-567.
Confined to New York, this article denounces the idea of a new party to solve local ills but advocates a committee to see that honest and efficient men are elected.

"The Constitutional Amendment on City Government," *Nation,* vol. 26 (February 14, 1878), pp. 108-109.
Points out the reasons why the amendment discussed is not likely to pass.

"The Prevention of Local Extravagance," *Nation,* vol. 21 (July 8, 1875), pp. 21-23.
A strong plea for state debt limitation in city government.

"The Rising Against the New Boss," *Nation,* vol. 21 (October 21, 1875), pp. 257-258.
The *Nation* was standing for John Kelley and protesting at what the papers were saying about him.

"The Science of Municipal Corruption," *Forum,* vol. 15 (March, 1893), pp. 43-51.

Weber, Gustavus A., "Improved Tenement Homes for American Cities," *Municipal Affairs,* vol. 1 (December, 1897), pp. 745-762.
An excellent account of tenements in the leading cities.

Wells, David A., "Reform of Local Taxation," *North American Review,* vol. 122 (April, 1876), pp. 357-403.
Applies chiefly to state questions; contains some worthwhile facts.

Welsh, Herbert, "A Definite Step Toward Municipal Reform," *Forum,* vol. 17 (April, 1894), pp. 179-185.
A survey of the origin and work of the first National Conference for Good City Government.

Wingate, Charles F., "An Episode in Municipal Government," *North American Review,* vol. 120 (January, 1875), pp. 119-174.
Covers the ring in New York City prior to 1875.

Wingate, Charles F., "An Episode in Municipal Government," *North American Review,* vol. 123 (October, 1876), pp. 362-425.
A good account of the fall of the Tweed Ring in New York.

Woodruff, Clinton Rogers, "A Year's Municipal Development," National Conference for Good City Government, *Proceedings for 1900,* pp. 67-87.
A very valuable statement.

Woodruff, Clinton Rogers, "The Progress of Municipal Reform," *Municipal Affairs,* vol. 1 (June, 1897), pp. 301-316.
An excellent survey of the civil service struggle and its accomplishments in general.

PAMPHLETS

Bradford, Gamaliel, *Our Failure in Municipal Government.* n. p., 1893.
Offers a good account of the failure of the framework of city government.

Committee on Press and Literature of the Citizens' Union of New York City, *Home Rule In Cities.* n. p., n. d.
Contains valuable excerpts from messages and committee resolutions on home rule for New York City.

Gladden, Washington, *The Salvation of the City.* Columbus, Ohio, 1894.

King, A. B., *The Political Mission of Tammany Hall.* New York, 1892.
An interesting discussion of the machine and the reformation of Tammany Hall.

Low, Seth, *The Problem of Municipal Government in the United States.* Ithaca, New York, 1887.
Mayor Low states the problem in a few words.

Rowe, L. S. and Welling, Richard W. G., *Reform in Municipal Government.* Boston, 1894.
Largely a comparison with European cities.

Shepard, Edward M., *The Competitive Test and The Civil Service of States and Cities.* New York, 1885.
Urges reform and explains the needs in civil service.

Shepherd, H. M., *The Mayor and The City.* n. p., 1894.
An excellent study of the decline of the Council and the Mayor's rise to power.

Wilby, Charles B., *Municipal Reform Impossible Under the Spoils System.* Chicago, 1894.
A paper read at the annual meeting of the National Civil Service Reform League, Chicago, 1894.

GOVERNMENT DOCUMENTS

Fassett Committee, *Testimony Taken Before the Senate Committees on Cities, Pursuant to Resolutions Adopted January 20, 1890.* 5 v. Albany, 1890.
An invaluable source.

Lexow Committee, *Report and Proceedings of the Senate Committee Appointed to Investigate the Police Department of the City of New York.* 5 v. Albany, 1895.
A mine of information.

Mazet Committee, *Report of the Special Committee of the Assembly Appointed to Investigate the Public Offices and Departments of the City of New York and the Counties Therein Included.* 5 v. Albany, 1900.
A very exhaustive report.

"Civil Service In the United States," 47th Congress, 1st Session, *Senate Report* No. 576 (May 15, 1882), pp. 1-225.
Contains Senate debates and shows how local pressure was influential in getting national civil service.

INTERVIEW

Interview with Mrs. Joseph W. Folk, June 2, 1937.

SECONDARY MATERIAL
BOOKS

Allinson, Edward Pease, and Penrose, Boies, *Philadelphia, 1681-1887: A History of Municipal Development.* Philadelphia, 1887.
  A very helpful source for the facts on the structure of Philadelphia city government.

Altman, Orven Roland, *Problems of Government in the St. Louis Metropolitan Area.* Urbana, Illinois, 1927.

Ashley, Percy, *Local and Central Government; A Comparative Study of England, France, Prussia and the United States.* New York and London, 1906.
  Important in making comparisons; contains an excellent chart comparing the Mayor and the President.

Bishop, Joseph Bucklin, *Theodore Roosevelt and His Time Shown in His Own Letters.* 2 v. New York, 1920.

Bogart, Ernest Ludlow, *Financial History of Ohio.* Champaign, Illinois, 1912.
  Contains some useful facts.

Brooks, R. C., *Corruption in American Politics and Life.* New York, 1910.
  A general study of corruption.

Brown, William G., *A History of Alabama.* New York, 1900.
  An elementary textbook; has a fair account of Mobile's struggle in 1878.

Bryce, James, *The American Commonwealth.* 2 v. New York, 1888, 1911.
  An invaluable and influential account of the conditions of American city government and the reform movement.

Castle, Henry Anson, *History of St. Paul and Vicinity.* 3 v. New York, 1912.
  The first volume contains a few points of interest.

Clow, Frederick Redman, *A Comparative Study of the Administration of City Finances in the United States.* New York, 1901.
  A very helpful study of city finance.

Conkling, Alfred Ronald, *City Government in the United States.* New York, 1899.
  Contains some good suggestions and facts.

DeWitt, Benjamin Parke, *The Progressive Movement: A Non-Partisan, Comprehensive Discussion of Current Tendencies in American Politics.* New York, 1925.

Dexter, Edwin Grant, *A History of Education in the United States.* New York, 1904.
Offers a thorough presentation of the education problem.

Durham, Nelson W., *History of the City of Spokane and Spokane County, Washington, from Its Earliest Settlement to the Present Time.* 3 v. Chicago, 1912.
The first volume alone is somewhat useful.

Eaton, Dorman B., *The Government of Municipalities.* New York, 1899.
A general survey of the author's attitude towards municipal government; denounces recent legislation for New York, bitterly attacks opponents of home rule.

Ely, Richard T., *Taxation in American States and Cities.* New York, 1888.
Good for facts and figures.

Ely, Richard T., *The Coming City.* New York, 1902.
Also useful for data.

Fairlie, John Archibald, *A Report on the Taxation and Revenue System of Illinois.* Danville, Illinois, 1910.
Offers some important facts recorded by a keen observer.

Fairlie, John Archibald, *The Centralization of Administration in New York State.* New York, 1898.
A very scholarly study.

Faulkner, Harold Underwood, *American Economic History.* New York, 1925.
Useful for a study of the growth of cities and related statistics.

Faulkner, Harold Underwood, *The Quest for Social Justice 1898-1914* (Arthur M. Schlesinger and Dixon Ryan Fox, eds., *A History of American Life,* vol. 11). New York, 1931.
An excellent survey and criticism in the chapter on "New Democracy."

Fish, C. R., *The Civil Service and the Patronage* (*Harvard Historical Studies,* vol. 11). New York, 1905.
An almost exhaustive study of the civil service movement in the United States.

Goodnow, Frank Johnson, *City Government in the United States.* New York, 1904.
Valuable for a general study of city government, but does not deal very much with the clash of forces for good government.

Goodnow, Frank Johnson, *Municipal Problems.* New York, 1907.
An excellent analysis of municipal problems.

Gregory, Charles Noble, *Civil Service Reform in American Municipali-*
ties. Iowa City, 1905.
A lecture before the Civic League in St. Louis about local civil service.

Griffith, Ernest S., *The Modern Development of City Government in*
the United Kingdom and in the United States. 2 v. London,
1927.
A comparison of American and British cities; gives an excellent analysis
of city government.

Hall, Clayton C., ed., *Baltimore: Its History and Its People.* 3 v. New
York, 1912.
The first volume is one of the best local histories.

Haynes, Fred E., *Social Politics in the United States.* New York, 1924.
Helpful for the background of reform movements.

Hennessy, Michael Edmund, *Twenty-Five Years of Massachusetts Poli-*
tics from Russell to McCall 1890-1915. Boston, 1917.
Deals with state politics and incidentally with city government.

Howe, Frederic C., *The City the Hope of Democracy.* New York, 1905.

Howe, Frederic C., *The Modern City and Its Problems.* New York,
1915.
A very interesting and worthwhile book.

King, Clyde Lyndon, *The History of the Government of Denver with*
Special References to its Relations with Public Service Corpora-
tions. Denver, 1911.
Wide in scope; contains some good accounts of city government.

Larned, Josephus Nelson, *A History of Buffalo, Delineating the Evolu-*
tion of the City. 2 v. New York, 1911.
The first volume contains some good facts.

Lee, Francis Bazley, *New Jersey as a Colony and as a State.* 4 v. New
York, 1902.
Last volume is somewhat useful.

Lyman, Robert Hunt, *The World Almanac and Book of Facts for*
1923.

Matthews, Nathan, *Municipal Charters; a Discussion of the Essentials*
of a City Charter, with Forms or Models for Adoption. Cambridge, 1914.
A valuable study of charter government by a former Mayor of Boston.

Merriam, Charles Edward, *Chicago A More Intimate View of Urban*
Politics. New York, 1929.
A valuable study of Chicago politics.

Merriam, Charles Edward, *Report of an Investigation of the Municipal Revenues of Chicago.* Chicago, 1906.
A splendid contribution to the study of city government finances.

Munro, William Bennett, *The Government of American Cities.* New York, 1912.
A scholarly piece of work, brilliantly written.

McBain, Howard Lee, *The Law and Practice of Municipal Home Rule.* New York, 1916.
A comprehensive and illuminating study of the home rule question.

Nevins, Allan, *The Emergence of Modern America 1865-1878* (Arthur M. Schlesinger and Dixon Ryan Fox, eds., *A History of American Life,* vol. 8). New York, 1927.
A number of chapters in this charming and illuminating book aid in the study of conditions and reforms to 1878.

Orth, Samuel Peter, *A History of Cleveland, Ohio.* 3 v. Cleveland, 1910.
The first volume is useful.

Orth, Samuel Peter, *The Boss and The Machine* (Allen Johnson, ed., *The Chronicles of America Series,* vol. 43). New Haven, 1920.
Confined chiefly to Tammany Hall.

Orth, Samuel Peter, *The Centralization of Administration in Ohio.* New York, 1903.
An excellent study of the struggle for home rule.

Patton, Odis Knight, *Home Rule in Iowa.* Iowa City, 1914.
Contains the story of home rule and special legislation in Iowa as well as in other states.

Reed, Thomas H., *Municipal Government in the United States.* New York, 1934.

Rice, James Montgomery, *Peoria City and County, Illinois; A Record of Settlement, Organization, Progress and Achievement.* Chicago, 1912.

Schlesinger, Arthur M., *New Viewpoints in American History.* New York, 1922.
A highly invaluable book for the study of new viewpoints. It gives many helpful suggestions about reform movements in general.

Schlesinger, Arthur M., *Political and Social History of the United States 1829-1925.* New York, 1925.
Helpful for a background study of the period and some facts on suffrage.

Schlesinger, Arthur M., *The Rise of the City 1878-1898* (Arthur M. Schlesinger and Dixon Ryan Fox, eds., *A History of American Life,* vol. 10). New York, 1933.
Emphasizes social and intellectual aspects.

Sparling, Samuel Edwin, *Municipal History and Present Organization of the City of Chicago.* Madison, Wis., 1898.
Particularly good for statistics.

Steffens, Lincoln, *The Struggle for Self-Government in the United States: Being an Attempt to Trace American Political Corruption to its Sources in Six States in the United States.* New York, 1906.

Story, Russell M., *The American Municipal Executive.* Urbana, Illinois, 1918.

Utley, Henry Munson and Cutcheon Byron M., *Michigan as a Province, Territory and State, the Twenty-Sixth Member of the Union,* 4 v. New York, 1906.
The last volume is very pertinent, especially the chapter on Mayor Pingree.

Weber, A. F., *The Growth of Cities in the Nineteenth Century.* New York, 1899.
A valuable statistical study of the cities of the world.

Werner, M. R., *Tammany Hall.* Garden City, New York, 1928.
A vivid account of the role of John Kelley and Richard Croker and their battle against reform.

Wilcox, Delos Franklin, *Municipal Government in Michigan and Ohio: A Study in the Relations of City and Commonwealth.* New York, 1896.
A thorough study of municipal government in Ohio and Michigan; especially helpful for facts about reform efforts.

Zink, Harold, *City Bosses in the United States: A Study of Twenty Municipal Bosses.* Durham, N. C., 1931.
One of the best books on the subject. Full of human interest; presents many aspects of city government.

ARTICLES

Agar, John G., "Legislative Interference in New York," *Municipal Affairs,* vol. 6 (June, 1902), pp. 198-211.
A good discussion of the causes of and remedies for state interference.

Allinson, Edward Pease, and Penrose, Boies, "The City Government of Philadelphia," Johns Hopkins University, *Studies in Historical and Political Science,* vol. 5 (January-February, 1887), pp. 7-72.

Blair, James L., "The St. Louis Disclosures," National Conference for Good City Government and the National Municipal League, *Proceedings for 1903,* pp. 87-108.

Bocock, John Paul, "The Irish Conquest of Our Cities," *Forum*, vol. 17 (April, 1894), pp. 186-195.
A most interesting account of the Irish influence and political power in American cities.

Browne, George Morgan, "Municipal Reform," *New Englander,* vol. 45 (February, 1886), pp. 152-160.

Deming, Horace E., "Municipal Nomination Reforms," American Academy of Political and Social Science, *Annals,* vol. 25 (March, 1905), pp. 203-217.
A brief but searching examination of the primary laws, especially those of New York.

Edmonds, Franklin Spencer, "Some Social Effects of a Reform Movement," American Academy of Political and Social Science, *Annals,* vol. 28 (November, 1906), pp. 405-410.
An excellent article by the Chairman of City Committee, Philadelphia. Shows social and economic values of reform, but does not prove its point conclusively.

Eliot, Charles W., "One Remedy for Municipal Misgovernment," *Forum,* vol. 12 (October, 1891), pp. 153-168.
Examines the causes of and remedies for faulty local government. Dr. Elliot does not think that immigration had much to do with the evils of city government.

Foulke, William Dudley, "Coming of Age: Municipal Progress in Twenty-One Years," *National Municipal Review,* vol. 5 (January, 1916), pp. 12-22.
Contains a good account of the reasons why cities were in such a deplorable state during the nineteenth century.

Fowler, B. O., "Twenty-Five Years of Bribery and Corrupt Practices," *Arena,* vol. 31 (January, 1904), pp. 12-49.
Deals chiefly with corruption in legislation regarding railroads.

Frederick, John H., "Edwin Henry Fitler," *Dictionary of American Biography,* vol. 6, pp. 431-432.

Hart, Albert Bushnell, "The Rise of American Cities," *The Quarterly Journal of Economics,* vol. 4 (January, 1890), pp. 129-157.

Higgins, Edward E., "Municipal and Private Management of Street Railways—A Study of Results and Possibilities," *Municipal Affairs,* vol. 1 (September, 1897), pp. 458-490.
Presents strong arguments against municipal ownership.

Howe, William W., "Municipal History of New Orleans," Johns Hopkins University, *Studies in Historical and Political Science,* vol. 7 (April, 1889), pp. 159-184.
Brief and abstract; a few statistics and facts are worthwhile.

Insley, Edward, "How to Reform the Primary-Election System," *Arena,* vol. 17 (June, 1897), pp. 1013-1023.
  An urgent appeal for mandatory primary laws and for strict enforcement of measures regulating primaries.

King, Hoyt, "The Reform Movement in Chicago," American Association of Political and Social Science, *Annals,* vol. 25 (March, 1905), pp. 33-45.
  Very helpful in pointing out the work of local reform organizations.

Larson, Lawrence Marcellus, "A Financial and Administrative History of Milwaukee," Bulletin of the University of Wisconsin, *Economic and Political Science Series,* vol. 4 (1908).
  Offers a very thorough study of the financial question.

Older, Mrs. Fremont, "The Story of a Reformer's Wife," *McClure's Magazine,* vol. 33 (July, 1909), pp. 277-293.

Porter, J. D., "The City of Washington: Its Origin and Administration," Johns Hopkins University, *Studies in Historical and Political Science,* vol. 3 (November and December, 1885).

Ralph, Julian, "Western Modes of City Management," *Harper's Magazine,* vol. 84 (April, 1892), pp. 709-721.

Reform Club Committee on City Affairs, "Street Railway Franchises in New York," *Municipal Affairs,* vol. 6 (March, 1902), pp. 68-86.
  Evidence exposing what had been done in granting franchises.

Snow, Marshall S., "The City Government of Saint Louis," Johns Hopkins University, *Studies in Historical and Political Science,* vol. 5 (April, 1887), pp. 141-174.
  A good survey of the struggle for the home rule charter of 1876.

"The Key To Municipal Reform," *Century,* vol. 42 (October, 1891), pp. 953, 954.
  Urges home rule for cities.

Van Doren, Mark, "Anthony Comstock," *Dictionary of American Biography,* vol. 4, pp. 330, 331.

Weber, A. F., "Rapid Transit and The Housing Problem," *Municipal Affairs,* vol. 6 (Fall, 1902), pp. 409-417.
  Some valuable statistics and facts.

Williamson, Mrs. Emily E., "Department of Philanthropy, Charities, and Social Problems," American Academy of Political and Social Science, *Annals,* vol. 25 (January, 1905), pp. 189-202.
  A fine survey of conditions in 1904 and some valuable facts on previous years.

Woodward, William C., "Some Problems in Municipal Sanitation, From an Executive Standpoint," *Journal of Social Science,* vol. 40 (December, 1902), pp. 132-139.

Wright, Andrew, "The Development of Park Systems in America," American Academy of Political and Social Science, *Annals,* vol. 25 (March, 1905), pp. 218-234.
A good account of the origin and growth of city planning.

Young, James T., "The Basis of Present Reform Movements," American Academy of Political and Social Science, *Annals,* vol. 29 (March, 1903), pp. 238-251.
A survey of the general phases of reform and the weaknesses in reform methods.

PAMPHLETS

Pease, Thomas Hunington, *The Selection of Municipal Officers: The Terms and Tenure.* Boston, 1884.

ILLUSTRATIONS

Survey Graphic, vol. 20 (October, 1931), pp. 7-41.

RUE COMPANY, *PRINTERS,* DENTON, MD,

SIGNIFICANT PUBLIC AFFAIRS STUDIES

RIVAL UNIONISM IN THE UNITED STATES—*Walter Galenson.* A thorough-going and impartial study of the history, development, programs, and techniques of rival unions. ($3.25 Cloth, $2.50 Paper).

THE COAL INDUSTRY: A STUDY IN SOCIAL CONTROL—*Glen Parker.* A comprehensive study. Introduction by Howard Gray. ($3 Cloth, $2.50 Paper).

GOVERNMENT SPENDING AND ECONOMIC EXPANSION—*Professors Arthur E. Burns and Donald S. Watson.* An analysis of government spending during the past decade. ($2.50 Cloth, $2 Paper).

THE AMERICAN LABOR PRESS: An Annotated Directory. Information about 677 papers and magazines. Introduction by John R. Commons. ($2).

MONETARY MANAGEMENT UNDER THE NEW DEAL—*Dr. Arthur W. Crawford.* A comprehensive and detailed study with critical commentary. ($3.75 Cloth, $3.25 Paper).

J. LAURENCE LAUGHLIN—*Alfred Bornemann.* A case study containing biographical notes. Introduction by L. C. Marshall. ($2.50 Cloth, $2 Paper).

BALLOT BEHAVIOR—*Louis H. Bean.* A new basis for political measurement and forecasting. Introduction by Charles E. Merriam. ($1.50 Cloth, $1 Paper).

INTERNATIONAL LAW AND AMERICAN TREATMENT OF ALIEN ENEMY PROPERTY—*James A. Gathings.* Introduction by Prof. Edwin Borchard. ($3 Cloth, $2.50 Paper).

PAMPHLETS

THE FUTURE OF THE BRITISH COMMONWEALTH OF NATIONS—*Theodore Kraft.* Introduction by Sir Willmott Lewis. (50c).

THE POLL TAX—*Dr. Frank P. Graham, Barry Bingham, Prof. H. C. Nixon and others.* A survey of the major aspects of the tax. (25c).

ANTI-TRUST LAW ENFORCEMENT, PAST AND FUTURE—*Thurman Arnold.* A statement concerning the basic problems. (25c).

IN DEFENSE OF DEMOCRACY—*Justice Frank Murphy.* A manifesto concerning civil liberties—with especial reference to the present war situation. Introductory notes by President Roosevelt and Dr. Charles A. Beard. (10c).

HITLER AND THE WAR—*Dr. Hermann Rauschning.* An analysis based upon the author's knowledge as Nazi President of the Danzig Senate. (10c).

TOTAL DEFENSE—*Report of the Committee on Economic Defense.* An examination of the economic problems which have arisen out of the war. (10c).

PUERTO RICAN PROBLEMS—*Dr. Gertrude C. Bussey, Prof. Paul T. Homan, Bailey W. Diffie and others* (10c).

FIVE YEARS OF HITLER—*Prof. Frederick Schuman, Rev. Henry Smith Leiper, Dr. Alice Hamilton, Prof. Robert Brady, Charles A. Beard.* (10c).

NATIONAL DEFENSE—*President Franklin D. Roosevelt.* A compilation of recent speeches and statements. Introduction by Senator Morris Sheppard. (10c).

DEMOCRATIC EDUCATION—*Progressive Education Association.* A nine-point program with regard to national defense. (25c).

ABSENTEE VOTING AND REGISTRATION—*Prof. James K. Pollock.* A detailed guide. Introduction by Howard P. Jones. (25c).

FIFTH COLUMN LESSONS FOR AMERICA—*Col. William Donovan and Edgar Mowrer.* An analysis based upon recent Nazi tactics. Introduction by Col. Frank Knox. (25c).

ITALIAN FASCIST ACTIVITIES IN THE U. S.—*Prof. Gaetano Salvemini.* A scholarly exposé. Introduction by Prof. William Y. Elliott. (25c).

AMERICAN COUNCIL ON PUBLIC AFFAIRS
1734 Eye Street, Washington, D. C.

39911